The Blueprint for Vibrant Health

A Guide to Healing the Mind, Body, and Spirit

Gina L. Spielman, LCSW, C.H.

Table of Contents

Disclaimer

Even though this book is highly likely to benefit a large number of people, it needs to be made clear that it is not a replacement for a relationship (or potential relationship) with any healthcare providers.

The author and publisher assume no liability for any possible harm caused by the reader that may result from the use of content contained in this publication, and recommend common sense when considering the described suggestions. Also, some of the information (such as website addresses and links) may have changed since publication.

Chapter One

Introduction

This exciting and informative book contains everything you need to know in order to naturally restore emotional, spiritual, and physical wellbeing. This is one of those publications that all of us can benefit from reading, especially those who have been diagnosed with a chronic condition and are open to alternative approaches. It shows countless ways to awaken your own innate healing power, which exists inside yourself, in order to overcome illness and unleash vibrant health. What most of the mainstream medical doctors are not telling you is that the human body has a tremendous ability to heal itself, especially when mental, physical, and spiritual health all come together. This book will address how psychological, physical/biological, and spiritual interventions can all unite for true healing and overall long-term health.

I am a professional psychotherapist and certified hypnotist with a Master's Degree and more than twenty five years of experience working in the healthcare field. I have continually learned effective holistic approaches by attending clinical professional trainings, becoming a Certified Mental Health Integrative Medicine Provider, and achieving Certification in Natural Holistic Remedies. In addition, due to my personal journey with autoimmune conditions, there is first-hand knowledge of my own healing ability. The experience with my own healthcare, and all of the service providers and healers I have learned from over the years, has helped solidify my knowledge. All of that background, along with extensive research, has merged to create this life-changing book.

At the time of this writing, it seems that unfortunately Western medicine has failed in many ways, especially with chronic complex diseases, and that will be discussed in this book. From my experience with autoimmune issues, in particular, mainstream medical doctors can order tests that may suggest a certain disease, but even after a definite diagnosis is made (sometimes years later), they usually fail on the treatment side of things. For chronic conditions, mainstream medical doctors often have surprisingly little to offer in ways of quality, safe treatment and real healing (focusing only on whether or not there is a drug available). Also, the scientific rigidity of Western medicine frequently dictates that many diseases are not treatable. Autoimmune diseases are what come to mind often, and are usually placed in the "untreatable" category by Western doctors. They often come across as having knowledge of certain conditions, some of which they actually know little about, giving messages such as "there's no treatment and also no way to prevent it". It is astounding to find that with many diseases, the "untreatable" mindset is only accepted by the "experts" of Western medicine. In this book, inspiring stories are offered, often necessary to help instill much needed hope in patients who have been told "there is nothing that can be done", by doctors (such as rheumatologists) who clearly do not know about natural holistic healing, may provide little encouragement, and sometimes behave like they cannot have these "untreatable" patients leave their offices quickly enough.

This book is also filled with psychological techniques that heal the mind, as well as the body, as studies are increasingly confirming strong mind-body links. Research continues to discover facts like the nervous and digestive systems are closely connected, hence your state of mind affects your gut and vice versa. New research is also revealing concerns such as gut bacteria issues causing increased anxiety and depression (biological factors contributing to psychological conditions). Many people are not aware of how the body has an amazing ability to heal itself, the power of the mind and spirit to heal the body, and how we can effectively use natural techniques and remedies. As Americans, we tend to use too many chemical medications that have the potential to harm us. This book can be an alternative to synthetic drugs as it teaches how you can access the wonderful healing ability of your body, as well as specific therapeutic remedies and activities. I include, among other things, why I believe we get sick and how to heal holistically. A few of the suggestions may be surprising (and some a bit controversial), such as using humor, releasing of negativity, and working with healing crystals and stones.

In addition, countless alternative healthcare suggestions are provided, such as incorporating supplements, as well as other natural treatments, remedies, and activities that are highly likely to help the therapeutic process. Also included is a fascinating interview with a professional hypnotherapist who treats physical disorders (such as autoimmune diseases) with hypnotherapy. It also contains highly educational and inspirational quotes from authors, healers, spiritual leaders, and health care providers. Several research studies are also touched upon.

My goal is to instill much needed optimism, especially at important times and crossroads for patients, such as when one is newly diagnosed. More than anything, I want readers to say to me "Because of your book I did not give up". I truly believe this publication will assist you in reaching your absolute highest potential. After all, knowledge is power!

"There is a healing force within each of us, a kind of divine physician seated within our minds and in communication with every cell of our being."

~ Marianne Williamson

Preventing illness will also be increasingly on the minds of Americans due to the fact that the healthcare system is changing dramatically. It is no longer a "given" that you will be able to receive coverage for your preferred healthcare providers, and if you do get coverage, the cost for you to see them will likely be higher (in the form of co-pays, co-insurance, and deductibles), and appointment time slots will be shorter. The overall cost-cutting of the entire United States medical system is going to require people to be much more involved in their own heath care. Therefore, using recommendations in this book (and beyond) in order to personally play a role in preventing and managing all health conditions will be more of a concern for many Americans. The fact that prescription-drug prices are spiking will more often direct patients to go the natural and preventative routes. In addition, if you are a health professional or healer, this book is something to consider for your patients and clients, as following the suggestions will likely bring about healing at a more rapid pace. At minimum, it is highly probable that they will be able to reduce their amounts of treatments, pharmaceuticals, or dosages.

Holistic Medicine is a general term which usually includes the mind, body, and spirit (the whole person), where the patient is an active participant in his or her own healthcare and natural interventions are used. I see healing as having many definitions. Body and mind healing of course, but also spiritual. Therefore, if you are able to gain spiritual healing only, I also consider that a success (and anyone who is reading this book can at least accomplish that goal).

In my work with health insurance companies, I have seen that they often require a considerable amount of data proving that a specific treatment is effective. If that evidence is too minimal (for example, a lack of large formal scientific studies), they most often will not cover the therapy. Sadly, I believe that many effective treatments are not accessed by those who need them due to that reason. Hypnosis and acupuncture are two types of treatments which come to mind. These are effective interventions that many times have not specifically been covered by insurance. Sometimes people are uninformed about treatments such as hypnosis and acupuncture simply because their health insurance does not cover them. Their insurance companies are requiring large research studies to "prove" treatment effectiveness. However, the practitioners of such modalities are too busy actually making people better to conduct multiple in-depth scientific research studies, and they already know it works. Also, remember that if Big-Pharma cannot make money on something then it does not get much attention, whether it is a natural treatment or a supplement. I also think there are attempts to control a situation or silence it, if it is something that can actually heal people and cause Big-Pharma (or other large organizations) to lose money or power. It is baffling to me that my insurance will gladly cover toxic chemical pills with potentially severe side effects but will not cover certain providers, tests, supplements, therapies, or procedures that would be (and have been) truly healing.

Anyway, regardless of all of that, I urge you to do everything you can to bring your health to a higher level! Whenever possible, engage in activities such as meditation, self-hypnosis, visualization, or prayer, as they boost the number of circulating immune cells throughout the body, helping to prevent many illnesses. They also lower the effects of stress, including helping to stabilize blood pressure and blood sugar. All of this assists the healing process as well as health maintenance. Also boost your emotional health by identifying and releasing feelings, as well as engaging in mindfulness, expressing gratitude, and focusing on optimistic thoughts about the future. Along the lines of diet, eating foods that are healthy for your particular body is important, regardless if you are "overweight" or not. If possible, get daily physical exercise (mild to moderate intensity is usually best). Also, I truly believe that taking excellent care of yourself can create a strong defense against negative energies emanating from other people. Take time daily to nurture your mind, body, and spirit. This will significantly improve the likelihood of a positive outcome in any battle against heart disease, cancer, diabetes, autoimmunity, allergies, infections, mental health concerns, addictions, and more. Always remember that you have the power to be and stay healthy because healing often comes from within.

If you are taking any synthetic medications, see if you can possibly minimize them. *Work with your physician* to reduce your dosages or eliminate as many as possible, meanwhile conducting your own research, following holistic healing suggestions in this publication, and working closely with a natural health treatment provider.

"In my medical training, we were not taught that the body knows how to heal itself. Yet it is equipped with natural self-repair mechanisms that repair broken bones, kill cancer cells, fight infections, prevent aging, and

maintain the homeostasis of the body. These mechanisms that can be
flipped on or off with thoughts, beliefs, and feelings that originate in the
mind. This is great news, because it means, in essence, that you can heal
yourself."

~ Lissa Rankin, MD

Of course, this book is not a guarantee of a cure for everyone for every illness, but always remember a miracle can happen (I have seen first-hand), and can happen to you! I know that if you complete many of the recommendations offered, do your own research, and work with your healthcare professional, it is highly likely you will at least experience a decrease in symptoms or stop the progression of disease. This book is for prevention as well. For example, if your blood work suggests a certain disorder, you have a genetic predisposition for a specific disease, or you feel your health is starting to decline, this book can help tremendously. Or if you are seeking just symptom management or reduction, it can also make those goals possible. In addition, if you simply just want to feel better or keep your current health, then this book can assist you as well.

"It is time for minds to open and bodies to heal. Read, learn, and explore
your innate healing abilities".

~ Bernie Siegel, M.D., author of "Love, Medicine and Miracles"

In a pursuit to restore my own health, I did what I always do when there is something I really want: I did all the research possible, read all the books I could get my hands on, sought out all the providers and healers that could truly help, and asked every question. No stone was left unturned. Finally, all the pieces of this complex "puzzle" are falling into place for me, and they can be for you as well!

Chapter Two

Alternatives to Western Medicine

Thankfully, alternative medical interventions are moving further to the forefront of health and wellness discussions. I notice it especially with younger people. They question diagnoses, treatments, and prognoses given. I also see them getting further involved with their own, as well as family members' healthcare, which is great! I am noticing an increased desire to raise insight as well as discover alternative pathways to self-awareness. More and more people are looking to explore wellness from all angles (mind, body, and spirit). This is a different perspective on health and healing here in the United States, and it is becoming more common. As you educate yourself, you will clearly see that it is not mysterious. It also keeps the power in your own hands. Health reflects your relationship with yourself, your body, and the world. From everything I have seen and read during my life, for the most part I do *not* believe in untreatable diseases. My viewpoint has evolved into illness showing up as an invitation to change your relationship with yourself, and the world around you, for the better.

One alternative healthcare approach is Integrative Medicine which is healing-oriented and takes account of the whole person holistically (body, mind, and spirit), including all aspects of lifestyle. It emphasizes the therapeutic relationship and utilizes all appropriate therapies, both alternative and conventional (Western) medicine.

The Functional Medicine model utilizes both Integrative Medicine and Holistic Medicine approaches. It organizes and applies knowledge in a systematic way, exploring the origins of disease and factors that have the potential to harm human health. This model does consider the diagnosis, but also seeks to answer the question of why the person has the illness. Discovering all of the antecedents, current triggers, and mediators that underlie symptoms, illness behaviors, and pathology all shines light on the answers using multiple lenses to view disease. The goal is returning the body, whose health is a result of its genetics and the environment in which these genetics have been immersed, to the highest possible functioning. Chronic diseases usually involve many organ systems, and a systematic method of viewing each case is required. Americans are experiencing a large increase in complex, chronic diseases, such as autoimmune disorders, diabetes, heart disease, cancer, and mental illness. The system of medicine currently practiced by most physicians in the United States is oriented toward acute care (the diagnosis and treatment of trauma or illness that is of short duration and in need of urgent care, such as a heart attack or a wound). Doctors then apply specific treatments such as pharmaceuticals or surgery treating the immediate problem or symptom. Unfortunately, the acute-care approach is not equipped to handle complex chronic disease. Often, the model does not evaluate the unique genetic makeup of each individual, and does not explore the aspects of today's modern lifestyle that have a direct influence on the rise in chronic disease in the United States (critical factors such as stress, effects of trauma, relationships, lifestyle, diet, and exposure to toxins). Most

Western medicine physicians are not adequately trained to assess the root causes of complex chronic disease, or involve interventions such as diet, exercise, and psychological help to both treat and prevent these illnesses in their patients. Functional Medicine is a different and powerful approach, with methodology and tools that are specifically designed to treat, heal, and prevent diseases, along with maintaining long-term health.

A Naturopathic Doctor uses a system of alternative medicine based on the theory that disease can usually be successfully treated or prevented (and health can be maintained) without the use of synthetic drugs. This approach uses holistic interventions and techniques such as diet improvements, supplement usage, stress management, exercise, and increased sleep. Linkages to additional treatments such as massage therapy and psychological counseling are also frequently utilized.

Acupuncture and Traditional Chinese Medicine (TCM) have countless benefits, too many to list in my opinion, but I will include some information.

In the past, I attended acupuncture treatments initially twice per week, and then eventually dropped down to about once per month. At first, I saw an amazing local acupuncturist. He has since moved to Utah and opened a new practice there. Currently, I see a new provider who has helped tremendously as well. In addition to her acupuncture services, she is quite knowledgeable about nutrient deficiencies and is often able to detect them. She also has high-quality supplements available in-office. Being well-informed about the complexities of the human immune system as well as the association between blood sugar fluctuations and adrenal health are additional highly beneficial attributes I have found in her. We have also worked on completing hair analysis testing. Having her for a treatment provider makes me feel like I have a knowledgeable and supportive ally on my side!

As far as my case goes, acupuncture and TCM have assisted with sleep, relaxation, pain and fatigue reduction, restoring hair growth, healthy lung functioning, circulation, digestive health, immune and hormone balancing, spiritual connection, mood enhancement, and more. The positive therapeutic relationship with the acupuncturist can also significantly help overall health, as with my experience.

TCM is based on the idea that vital energy (qi) flows through the body along pathways called meridians. In acupuncture, a practitioner inserts needles into the skin at points of the body that correspond with specific organs and meridians. Western research suggests that this activates natural painkillers in the brain. According to TCM, the process improves functioning by correcting energy blocks or imbalances in the organs. Studies have confirmed that the meridians (and acupuncture points) have several biophysical properties, which are quite different from non-acupuncture points.

Research is increasingly indicating that acupuncture is useful for numerous conditions, including chronic pain, nausea, anxiety, depression, and medication side effects. Studies confirm that acupuncture produces physical responses in the nerve cells, pituitary gland, and brain. The body then releases hormones, proteins, and brain "chemicals" that control several bodily functions. By these actions, acupuncture has the ability to positively influence blood pressure, immune system health, and more. Interestingly, preliminary scientific studies are finding specific TCM interventions to be useful and effective during cancer treatment.

Autoimmune disorders occur when there is imbalance in the body, according to TCM. This can originate from an excess or deficiency of yin and yang which can block the healthy flow of qi throughout the body. Acupuncture is used to assist in restoring balance, treating the root cause(s), meanwhile addressing symptoms unique to each autoimmune patient.

"The basis of acupuncture is expressed in this famous Chinese saying:

'Bu tong ze tong, tong ze bu tong' which means 'free flow: no pain, no free

flow: pain.' In other words, any kind of pain or illness represents an

obstruction in the normal flow of Qi or life force. Simply put, acupuncture

moves Qi, restoring free flow."

~ Kurt Redmond, L.Ac.

In TCM, the plan to treat and manage complex conditions such as an autoimmune disorder likely involves a combination of therapies and recommendations in addition to the acupuncture treatments. These often include stress-reducing exercises and therapies, moderate physical activity, nutrition consultation, supplements, Chinese medicine herbals, essential oils (all as tolerated and tailored to particular needs), bodywork or massage therapy, psychotherapy, hypnosis, and spiritual teachings.

During the assessment with a licensed acupuncturist, there will likely be a questionnaire for you to list your concerns, how they are affecting your life, and to what degree. The practitioner will then ask about your symptoms, health, history, and lifestyle. He or she will check your pulse and tongue, as well as other parts of the body. Knowledge will be gained on the health of your organs and glands, where qi has become blocked or imbalanced, and the state of your overall health. In general, treatment goals include eliminating symptoms, while addressing the root cause(s) and underlying imbalances affecting the quality and quantity of qi (which directly effects health and wellbeing). Acupuncture is a natural and safe way to assist your body's innate healing ability, as well as improve organ health and bring the body back into balance.

- Also see "Dan tien" chapter for more on TCM.

Chiropractic treatments by a skilled chiropractor could be a beneficial add-on to your recovery program. Chiropractic adjustments can help your hormones and all the chemicals in your body "auto correct", restoring the balance (hormones, endocrine system, and more). Some chiropractors have methods to address specific issues such as neuropathy or chronic pain. Most usually have the ability perform various tests in order to help identify any other issues which may be contributing to illness (examples would be an infection, nutrient deficiency, or allergy). They also usually have high-quality supplements available (in office) and help with selection. In addition, chiropractors address important issues such as proper posture, which has been known to benefit overall health.

Several years ago, I was disappointed in the lack of assistance from Western medicine and was frequently wondering "What else can help?" Therefore I started seeing a chiropractor. After consultations, chiropractic adjustments, extensive high-quality allergy testing (eliminating allergens calms down the immune system in a positive way), lab work, and beginning several quality supplements (Omega-3 essential fatty acids, probiotics, vitamins/minerals, and L-Glutamine), I was feeling much better. So much better that we decided to try and have a child. Then I got pregnant immediately and the pregnancy was healthy, giving birth to an awesome baby boy. I did then see a chiropractic internist later on which took it all a bit further and helped with some additional concerns. This included more lab tests, dietary changes, and specific supplements.

With alternative approaches, conditions can be caught much earlier, giving enough time to reverse illness and prevent an actual diagnosis. Western medicine is not well known for prevention of disease, or detection of a disease developing. I am sure many of you have been baffled after years of seeing Western medical doctors who seem to have no real explanation for your symptoms. Often, their tests only detect a severe problem, and at that point the illness has usually progressed. For just one example, an acupuncturist can usually see a kidney issue before Western medicine would discover it. Conditions which are caught early are often much easier to treat. Also, for some reason, many Western medical doctors seem to not believe in, or understand the value of, bringing the body back into balance.

It is important to note that *"The Journal of Alternative and Complementary Medicine: Research on Paradigm, Practice, and Policy"* is a leading peer-reviewed journal providing scientific data for the assessment and incorporation of complementary and alternative approaches into mainstream medicine. The journal provides original research that directly impacts patient therapies, protocols, and strategies. The ultimate goal of the journal is to improve the quality of healing.

If you have a disease, or health concerns, and your only choice is a mainstream medical doctor, then at the very least, ask if he or she is willing to work with you and study complementary and alternative approaches.

I encourage you to consider all treatment possibilities for yourself and research Functional Medicine, Integrative, TCM, Ayurvedic, Chiropractic care, and Naturopathy. All of those systems are similar in that they seek to treat and heal the underlying causes rather than just the symptoms. The providers typically spend more time with patients and see the person as "whole" and unique. You owe it to yourself to be well informed and health-empowered! If you have an illness, I urge you to be followed by at least one of these types of practitioners.

Here are some websites that have listings of natural, Functional, Integrative, holistic, and TCM practitioners:

- Naturopathic.org

- FunctionalMedicine.org

- IntegrativeMedicineForMentalHealth.com

- Chirodirectory.com

- Osteopathic.org

- Acufinder.com

It is also important to note that sometimes health insurance covers alternative treatments.

"We are already in the midst of a very slow shift in medicine, propelled by consumers who are seeking out complementary medicine practitioners in record numbers. It's been a long time coming, but the quantum biological revolution is almost here."

~ Bruce H. Lipton, Ph.D

As a side note, some people are a bit concerned that, like many mainstream medical doctors, some alternative medicine practitioners place too much emphasis on expensive tests and too little on self-care (the most important and affordable remedy). "Functional medicine as a concept is an important step forward," says Dr. James Gordon, Integrative Medicine specialist and founder of the Center for Mind-Body Medicine. "However, some practitioners do a lot of tests and prescribe a lot of supplements and work on cleaning out the gut, but neglect the psychological, spiritual and social issues. That concerns me." Yes, it is true that people need to be educated on all aspects of healing, and I am telling you that this all-inclusive book is the answer! I do also have to add that tests done by a natural or alternative type of doctor can get quite pricey (and are not always paid by insurance). Therefore, it is a good idea to take control of your own healthcare knowing all of the costs upfront, and then of course taking excellent care of yourself in the meantime.

If you have a serious illness, I urge you to keep in mind that having optimism and a positive outlook helps everything! To give you some encouragement, let me tell you that my former acupuncturist has seen a reversing of chronic severe illnesses, and recoveries from diseases such as lupus and rheumatoid arthritis (RA). He has also treated (and studied) cases of scleroderma (serious autoimmune disease) that have reversed and also ones where the progression of the disease has ceased. My current acupuncturist has seen cases of severe connective tissue autoimmune disease go into long-term remission (where there are few or no symptoms) after some time using holistic interventions, lifestyle changes, and behavioral modifications. There are hypnotherapists that practice using a certain program that treats physical conditions (such as autoimmune diseases) bringing the patient to the point where the symptoms are no longer present. A fascinating interview with the creator of that program is included towards the end of this book. We all have also heard of other miraculous cases where people have cured themselves or healed from serious illnesses (such as cancer). In addition, we all know stories of patients diagnosed with certain "fatal" diseases living <u>much</u> longer than expected. During my research, I interviewed a woman who was diagnosed with lupus and then after implementing lifestyle changes and behavioral modifications, tested "negative". At the time of writing this book, she has virtually no symptoms. Her story (interview) is also included towards the end of this book.

"All things are possible."

~ Matthew 13:16

Chapter Three

Information on Autoimmune Diseases

Before I get too far with additional suggestions for healing, I wanted to touch upon autoimmune conditions specifically, as they are one large group of growing chronic issues that Western medicine typically does not do well in treating, in my opinion.

What causes autoimmune diseases? After personal experience dealing with my own autoimmune conditions, as well as looking at all of the work and research I have done, here are what I believe to be probable causes or contributors, in no particular order (if you have an autoimmune disease, it is likely that several of the below factors have come together to create the condition):

- Toxins and environmental factors (such as heavy metals, pesticides, pollution, chemicals)
- Effects of the modern world (such as high stress, lack of community, fast pace, technology)

- Lack of exercise or movement
- Diet (eating foods that are not healthy for one's particular body; not enough nutrient-dense foods)
- Leaky gut syndrome
- Genetic predisposition/family history
- Hormone imbalances
- Chronic infections (such as bacteria, yeast, viruses, dormant viruses)
- Unresolved emotional trauma (does not have to be life-threatening) and negative thought patterns (can be subconscious)
- Resentments, guilt, lack of self-love, difficulty receiving and giving love
- Spiritual interference and disconnect from "Source"
- Highly "sensitive" personality traits
- The "hygiene hypothesis" (where one's environment has been too clean)

Living with illness is challenging enough but dealing with an autoimmune disease can be even more difficult in some ways. Autoimmunity is still highly misunderstood by most people, including mainstream medical professionals. Those with autoimmune conditions often experience vague symptoms that can make diagnosing difficult. Treatments vary, and in many cases may need to rely entirely on behavioral and lifestyle changes, along with alternative interventions.

Here I will provide some key points regarding autoimmune conditions:

Autoimmune diseases essentially cause a person's body to "attack" what seem to be normal cells, in most cases. Our immune systems are comprised of a complex set of cells and organs that fight foreign invaders. In a healthy person, the body understands the difference between cells that are one's own and therefore safe, and those that need fighting off. In a person with autoimmune disease, the immune system is out of balance. The result can seem like a misguided attack on one's own body, which may negatively affect multiple physical functions and organs.

There are more than eighty types of autoimmune diseases. A small sampling of autoimmune conditions includes lupus, RA, Celiac disease, Crohn's disease, scleroderma, and psoriasis. Some examples of additional disorders thought to be related to autoimmunity include chronic fatigue syndrome, narcolepsy, and autism. I think we also might start finding that many other diseases are falling into the autoimmune "camp" or are a result of a "faulty" immune system.

Autoimmune diseases are relatively common. The American Autoimmune Related Diseases Association (AARDA) currently estimates that the number of Americans affected by an autoimmune disease is close to fifty million. Some even say that it is over fifty million (and a few others say it is well over fifty million). Specific autoimmune diseases, however, can be rare.

Symptoms of autoimmune diseases are sometimes confused with allergic reactions. There is some evidence linking genetic predisposition for both allergies and autoimmune conditions, and even suggesting that allergies can be a trigger for autoimmunity, however the two are quite different. Celiac disease is an example: A person with a gluten allergy and a person with Celiac would both need to remove dietary gluten. However, the body of the person with just the allergy is not "attacking" itself, and it is not a disease. He or she is not at the same amount of risk of intestinal damage, nutritional deficiencies, and other conditions associated with autoimmunity and Celiac (such as additional autoimmune diagnoses as well as GI cancer).

They can be genetic (or contain a family history component). Evidence suggests family members are more likely to develop the same or similar autoimmune conditions. However, genes and family history are not the whole picture. Other factors (likely from the previous list) contribute to the triggering of an autoimmune disease in a person with a genetic predisposition or family history.

They can take many years to formally diagnose. Because many autoimmune diseases affect various parts of the body across specialties, some symptoms may come and go, and there are good days and bad days, these conditions can be difficult for even medical experts to recognize and consequently treat, according to the AARDA. In many cases, there is no single test a doctor can order to confirm a diagnosis. Rather, tests either suggest a certain condition or rule out others. It is common for someone with an autoimmune disease to receive a general diagnosis first (such as IBS), or to be told the symptoms are just due to stress. In addition, sometimes visible symptoms must be present for some diagnoses to be made, such as what is frequently the case with scleroderma. This can make diagnosing quite difficult for those who have only internal symptoms such as GI distress.

"The much more mysterious action of our immune system is really the key to human health, and that system appears to play a key role in everything from allergies to obesity to cancer."

~ Alison Gopnik, "Mind & Matter" Author (Wall Street Journal)

Another interesting fact to note is that new research is also showing a link between Alzheimer's and faulty immune system functioning. This supplies more evidence supporting the idea that a properly functioning immune system really is the "key to human health".

Chapter Four

More about Causes

What actually is at the root of the imbalances that lead to most illnesses and disease? Is it food, our environment, or genetics? Those factors can all be important, yes. However, what research is pointing towards now is that no matter how perfect your diet is or how often you exercise, if you are experiencing negative stress all the time, illness is much more likely to be triggered. Science seems to be indicating that stress might be the number one cause of health problems and could be the root of most diseases. To keep it simple, negative stress overloads the body with harmful "chemicals" that break down the immune system, which then creates an environment for illness and disease to enter. If one is continually in the "fight-or-flight" mode, it can trigger markers in the body which lead to disease, even terminal illness.

The good news is that I believe most people have the capacity to heal. As you become skilled at managing stress, you can more easily take back control over your health and wellbeing. Do not remain in a "fear mode" over the percentages and types of carbohydrates, proteins, fats, raw foods, and cooked foods in your diet while discounting the effects of the emotional stress in your life and resulting mental wellbeing. Yes, eating fresh, natural, nutrient-dense foods that are right for your particular body is extremely beneficial for your overall health. However, consuming a high-quality diet while emotionally balanced and serene is a far superior path. My experience and research over the years have all convinced me that no other factor has more influence over health. Nutrition, exercise, and sleep are all important. However, emotional stress is one of the most significant root causes of chronic health problems. It is difficult for the body to defend against the damage that negative emotional stress creates over time. Your body actually pays a physical price when you feel angry or fearful (especially if left unprocessed). There is really no need to provide a list of health conditions that are caused by negative emotional stress, because almost every one is at least partly caused by it. This is exacerbated when unhealthy substances and behaviors are used for "coping". Emotional stress equals increased output by the sympathetic nervous system (accelerates heart rate, increases blood pressure, and constricts blood vessels), which then can cause a breakdown of tissues as well as accelerated aging. Stress management is an extremely important part of maintaining a healthy endocrine system. Stress can create hormone overproduction, which tends to lead to the malfunction of endocrine organs. Prolonged negative stress not only leads to fatigue, depression, and mental health concerns, but also a weakened and unhealthy immune system. This of course opens the door to a host of serious physical ailments.

"Stress will make your cholesterol go up,.. Without a doubt, that has been under recognized".

~ Stephen Kopecky, Cardiologist at Mayo Clinic

When under stress, muscles usually contract and tense up, negatively affecting blood vessels, nerves, organs, skin, and bones. If muscle tension is ongoing, it can result in a variety of musculoskeletal issues, including pain and muscle spasms.

"...negative attitudes such as suppressed anger/ rage, inability to forgive, resentfulness, holding grudges, etc. all stresses the adrenal glands and increases cortisol levels leading to adrenal exhaustion."

~ Jeremy E. Kaslow, M.D., F.A.C.P., F.A.C.A.A.I.

Some Fascinating Facts about the Initial Physical Effects of Emotional Stress:

- The digestive system slows, or shuts down, in order to use blood, nutrients, and oxygen for "fight-or-flight".
- Cortisol from adrenal glands is released to increase blood sugar and create a short burst of energy.
- Adrenal glands release epinephrine and norepinephrine to boost blood sugar and cardiac output.

- Most of the blood supply is sent to large muscle groups for "fight-or-flight".

- Heart rates and breathing increase, to supply more oxygen and nutrients to muscles.

- Pupil diameter enlarges which allows more light to enter eyes, and enhances vision, for fighting and running quickly in any type of environment.

Some Longer-Term Effects of Emotional Stress:

- Increased blood pressure, cholesterol, and heart attack risk.

- Lower bone density.

- Reduced ability for the immune system to fight off and recover from illness.

- Abdominal cramping, reflux, and nausea.

- Loss of libido, lower sperm count, and increased menstrual pain.

- Joint and muscle aches and pains.

- Headaches.

- Mental health concerns (including anxiety disorders, insomnia, anger, irritability, depression, lack of energy, and concentration issues).

Stress usually begins with your thoughts, which significantly impact how you feel (both physically and emotionally). Psychoneuroimmunology (PNI) is the fascinating study of the interaction between psychological processes and the nervous and immune systems. PNI is interdisciplinary, integrating psychiatry, psychology, neuroscience, immunology, physiology, genetics, pharmacology, biology, infectious diseases, rheumatology, and endocrinology. Key interests of PNI are in the communications between the nervous and immune systems, and the connections linking mental processes and health. PNI researches the physiological functioning of the neuroimmune system in health and disease, disorders of the neuroimmune system (such as immune system conditions, hypersensitivities, neuropathies, and more), and the physical and chemical characteristics of all components of the neuroimmune system.

When thoughts create strong emotions, the brain releases hormones that spread the information to every bodily system. Called neuropeptides, these hormones are informational molecules that bring messages to any cell that has receptors. When you have "negative" or what some call "lower" thoughts (such as ones which create fear, anxiety, anger, depression, or frustration), you can begin to trigger strong physical responses within the body. The more intense, negative, frequent, and chronic these thoughts are, the more likely they are to manifest physically in detrimental ways, especially if this is happening outside of awareness.

After knowing the facts, we clearly see that the mind has a strong influence on the physical body. While it is not possible to remove every single external source of stress, going within and learning successful coping skills as well as increasing emotional health, are things everyone can accomplish. We all need to take time for ourselves and cultivate positive energy in order to effectively handle stress. Several upcoming chapters in this book contain recommendations for meeting your goals in this arena. It is crucial for all of us to look within and take some time to understand what core beliefs are not working and clear that mental programming in order to regain power over our lives. One of the main reasons I have written this book is for you to become proficient in resolving and managing stress, which again I believe to be the root cause of health problems. I truly think it can be a life saver and am pleased you are taking a look. Working on this aspect is essential in the pathway of restoring your health and well-being.

This modern world can be a rough place to live, particularly if you are not paying attention to your own needs, what is truly important, and the positive aspects of life. I believe this type of situation is prime breeding ground for illness. Negative or lower thought patterns are fuel for disease. According to the CDC (Centers for Disease Control), there is an emotional component in eighty five percent of all illnesses. But you can rewire your subconscious mind to bring it back into balance, creating lasting health. It does take time to re-condition the mind to automatically have positive thoughts in most situations, but it will happen! Keep working and it will come, along with the healing that follows. I had scores of years with some negative thought patterns and was able to change significantly in just a few months. I continue to grow, learn, transform, and evolve. Of course there are exceptions to the rule. Obviously positive thoughts cannot accomplish the impossible such as altering existing chromosomes, but with most ailments, long-term positive thought patterns will improve overall health. Therefore, I urge you to look at your world with completely new eyes and really see the beauty of life!

"If you aren't amazed most of the time you aren't paying attention"

~ Michael Lipsey

Chapter Five

Rest and Relaxation are Absolutely Essential

I know it sounds so simple, but it needs to be emphasized that getting enough rest and relaxation is absolutely crucial for your overall health and healing. Americans are notorious for not getting enough down-time.

Your body needs a break, first and foremost. Doing all you can to participate in relaxation and rest also demonstrates the all-important action of self-love. Take at least one full day out of each week for rest, rejuvenation, and leisure activities allowing your mind and body to recover. In addition, I urge you to spend some time resting every afternoon (or whenever you can fit it in) doing activities such as napping, meditation, prayer, and so on.

Do whatever you can to get at least six to eight hours of restorative sleep every night in order to reduce stress, keep your body balanced, and decrease pain. Aim for nine hours whenever possible, as the body heals while sleeping. Sleep plays a huge role (one of the most important) in overall physical and emotional health. It helps the brain function, reduces the risk of chronic disease, promotes mental well-being, boosts immune system health, and much more. Studies also show that lack of sleep is associated with increased hunger and appetite, linking sleep loss with an increased risk of obesity. It is known that people tend to eat unhealthier foods, and more of them, when they do not get enough sleep. Research also shows that the more sleep you get, the lower your annual medical costs. Yet most people in this country are not getting enough sleep. Remember that lack of sleep and stress may cause some glands to malfunction. The good news is that if you begin following many of the recommendations in this book, most likely your ability to get some rest will improve.

Use positive affirmations such as "I deserve complete relaxation and rest", giving yourself permission to relax and sleep. The affirmation "I am so sleepy right now" works well while trying to fall asleep. You can add "I am dreaming" which can help as well. Continually repeating meditations is going to be beneficial. Be sure to spend some time unwinding before bed, doing activities that relax you (and know what those specific activities are). If you find yourself ruminating while trying to sleep (worrying and thinking about all of your tasks and troubles), keep repeating the following helpful affirmation given to me by my spiritual counselor: "Everything is exactly the way it's supposed to be right now even if I don't yet understand it". You can also assure yourself "I will revisit this during waking hours", and have a pen and paper by your bed to jot down anything that will need your attention later on. This will help release it from your mind so you can go back to sleep with no worries.

Using wording such as "I surrender" can also assist in falling asleep. The act of surrendering to the heavens, God, "Source", or whatever you feel positively connected with, while relaxing every part of the body, can bring a feeling of great peace. Adding the phrases "What will be, will be" and "I trust in the path of life" can also bring calm and tranquility.

Try imagining yourself as a ragdoll, heavy, weighing down into the bed. Use whatever imagery comes to mind and helps you the most. Also beneficial are affirmation statements such as "Relaxation is essential for my health" and "There is nothing I need to be doing right now other than resting".

Visualizing your participation in a mundane task can also lure you to sleep. Sometimes I think of an activity such as vacuuming or cleaning, and the simple back and forth repetitive movement makes me fall asleep. Visualizing a blank movie screen can also be helpful.

Maintain a routine sleep schedule and make your bedroom a sanctuary, away from any stress. Get room-darkening shades or wear a comfy sleep mask. Pay close attention to everything that helps you to fall into a deep restorative sleep, and keep participating in those activities. This usually means no screen time at night (or at least using blue light blocking computer glasses), and a television-free bedroom. Practicing excellent "sleep hygiene" will give your body more of an opportunity to strengthen and heal.

At a risk of being the "bearer of bad news", caffeine can be considered a drug. If you consume caffeine, and you are having any kind of sleep disruption, energy crashes during the day, or anxiety-type symptoms (including heart palpitations), then consider eliminating caffeine for a week to see if there is any improvement with your sleep, energy levels, or anxiety. Caffeine can affect the body for up two days. A week off will likely give you the answer you need. After a few caffeine-free days, withdrawal symptoms should be gone. You can replace your morning coffee with a delicious and healthy cup of herbal tea, or other alternative. I had to do this years ago when told by my healthcare providers to avoid coffee due to my health conditions. At first I felt angry about having to give up coffee, but then after a few days I did not miss it much anymore and actually felt better overall. So, even though coffee might be beneficial for some people, as far as my case goes, chamomile tea, and a few other teas derived from herbs and/or spices, are much healthier for me on a daily basis, and are more relaxing as well as nurturing. In addition, Gualala Roast is an example of a delicious coffee alternative that is caffeine-free and actually provides health benefits. It is available online.

Consuming a bit of cherry juice on a daily basis can also help your sleep. Researchers have shown it decreases inflammation and pain, as well as increases circulation, and improves sleep. In addition to essential nutrients, it contains high levels of melatonin (critical for sleep). There was a study (published in the "European Journal of Nutrition", Dec. 2012; 51(8):909-16) in which twenty healthy people drank either a placebo or tart cherry juice (from the Montmorency variety) for seven days. Among those who drank the cherry juice, the total melatonin content in their urine was significantly elevated. Also, the "actigraphy" (which is a sensor that monitors sleep and wake cycles) and daily diaries of their sleeping patterns showed that participants who consumed the cherry juice saw an increase of around fifteen minutes to the time spent in bed, twenty five minutes in their total sleep time, and a 5-6% increase in their "sleep efficiency" (a measure of sleep quality). I drink cherry juice very watered-down or add a bit to my fruit smoothies. Try it with cold fizzy water for an anti-inflammatory summer evening treat! I also like fresh pressed pure black cherry juice (watered down as well). Often, I eat whole fresh cherries whenever I can get my hands on them. Research is also finding that eating kiwi fruit an hour before bedtime seems to have similar positive effects on sleep (kiwi fruits are also easy to store long-term in the refrigerator). On a related note about sleep, Omega-3 fatty acids (found in supplement form as well as some foods) are essential for supporting melatonin production.

It is important to make sure you continuously have healthy levels of all essential vitamins and minerals in your body. For just one example, keeping healthy magnesium levels is crucial for restful restorative sleep.

Working out during the day will likely help you sleep longer and have a better night's rest, according to research. It also increases endorphins which make you happy! In addition, exposing your eyes to sunlight in the morning can help you fall asleep later that night. Open your blinds and turn on your lights as soon as you wake up. Take a walk outside in the morning and over your lunch hour (you will get exercise and healing light at the same time). If you have a window anywhere in your office, position your desk so that you are closer to it in order to receive maximum benefits from the natural light.

A weighted blanket can be helpful for sleep issues and anxiety (among other conditions) and is something to research as well. It can be used for all ages.

Emotional Freedom Techniques (EFT) have been known to help with falling asleep. While in bed, you can mentally tap (without actually using your hands) and think the "tapping phrases" in your mind. You can focus on statements such as "I am dozing off to sleep" or "I deserve deep restorative sleep".

- Also see the "Emotional Freedom Techniques (EFT)" chapter for more information.

After a tip from my current acupuncturist, I discovered that blood sugar fluctuations may interfere with getting enough rest. If you find you are waking up in the middle of the night or way too early in the morning and having difficulty falling back asleep (even after following recommendations in this chapter and beyond), it may be that your blood sugar has dramatically dropped, which can actually wake you up and keep you awake for a while. Help remedy that problem by managing blood sugar during the day and before bedtime (with interventions such as diet, exercise, stress management, and other suggestions in this book). This can all help the body be more balanced and calm, as well as prevent the "roller coaster" effect of blood sugar fluctuations.

Some medications can also cause sleep interruptions. If you think you could be in that type of situation, do your research, review with your healthcare provider, and come up with a solution. Interestingly, according to Michael Lara, MD, even pharmaceuticals directly aimed at inducing sleep do not actually bring a person to stage four sleep, which is the most restorative stage.

"If you suffer from insomnia, I really encourage you to try a drug-free option first, starting with cognitive behavioral therapy, which has been shown to help people fall asleep faster than prescription sleeping pills do."

~ Dr. Mike Dow

Chapter Six

Humor and Play

L augh often and have a sense of humor as much as possible. Do not take your life or yourself too seriously! Lighten-up and loosen-up!

"Your body cannot heal without play. Your mind cannot heal without laughter. Your soul cannot heal without joy."

~ Catherine Rippenger Fenwick

Interestingly, a significant amount of formal research has been done finding the act of laughing to be highly beneficial to the mind and body. Studies show that laughter increases overall immune system health. It also improves breathing, arterial blood flow, digestion, and sleep. In addition, it adjusts blood pressure and blood sugar, relaxes muscles, reduces pain, and actually burns calories. Laughter also alleviates inflammation, reduces stress (and cortisol levels), and improves memory. All of these findings point towards seriously considering humor in health, wellness, and treatment programs, as it could be used as a therapy. It can actually offer a pleasant addition to treatment plans for patients with physical conditions such as hypertension, diabetes, and heart problems. Laughter Yoga is actually a real thing and something to consider exploring as well.

"When we laugh, the stress hormone, cortisol, decreases and thus, our short-term memory will improve."

~ Dr. Mark Reeves

As an additional benefit, in most situations, laughter is more socially acceptable than crying and it is wonderfully contagious. So, be sure to take time out of every day to be child-like!

Humor tip: My husband had the idea of opening up a social media account with the only goal of following comedians he enjoys. Therefore, now anytime he logs in, he is amused in less than a minute. Try that idea, or one similar to that, and use it whenever you feel the need to laugh or be entertained!

"Laugh. Laugh till your side hurts! Surround yourself with people that do. It's compatible with every drug, and there are no side effects whatsoever!"

~ Joan Aubele, Author of "The Dance: A Story of Love, Faith, and Survival"

In addition, research suggests that anticipating a positive event can decrease the effects of detrimental stress hormones. Therefore, it is important to plan enjoyable activities as much as possible!

Live carefree! Pay attention to your body and what it needs. If you find yourself tightening up (and pay attention so you know when it is happening), then you can begin some relaxation exercises, meditations, humor, or affirmations allowing yourself to loosen up instantly.

"Simply put, daily doses of laughter are a very powerful healing force that can actually activate the wellness process"

~ Sidney H. Levinsohn, R. Ph.

Chapter Seven

Exercise

As soon as you are well enough, start an exercise program and get moving! Regular exercise is one of the pillars of vibrant health. It is not a secret that there are countless proven benefits. It improves sleep, helps eliminate general aches and pains, enhances mood, and boosts self-esteem. It increases cardiovascular health and muscle mass, lowers blood pressure, helps control body weight and blood sugar issues, aids in detoxification, and defends against a variety of diseases. Just like a nutritious diet, exercise promotes overall health and a balanced healthy immune system. It may contribute even more directly by promoting good circulation, which allows the cells and substances of the immune system to move throughout the body freely and work more efficiently. Regular exercise also prevents bone loss. Based on research, there are numerous overall benefits to exercise (physiological, social, and psychological) and few adverse effects. Exercise can also immediately produce positive results (such as decreasing depression and anxiety), which is great for those wanting instant gratification!

If needed, start slowly with walking or gentle stretching. The bottom line is that you have to move every day, and throughout the day. This is absolutely necessary for overall health and wellness. Yes, you need to rest on a daily basis, but researchers have found that lifestyles that are too sedentary are associated with greater risk for at least thirty-five chronic diseases and health conditions.

Be sure to break up your activity all throughout the day. Sitting or standing for long periods of time will both have a negative impact on your health. According to Michael Lara, MD, time spent sitting is associated with increased markers for inflammation. He has suggested that for every hour spent sitting, get up and walk for two minutes, and continue this throughout each day.

Just twenty-five minutes of brisk walking a day could add up to seven years to your life, according to heart experts. Researchers say moderate exercise could halve the risk of heart attack death among those in their fifties and sixties. New research suggests that regular exercise can delay the aging process. Sanjay Sharma, professor of inherited cardiac diseases in sports cardiology at St George's University Hospitals NHS Foundation Trust in London, said: "When you exercise moderately, you reduce your risk of dying from a heart attack when you're in your 50s and 60s by 50 per cent. That's a really big deal." Everyone should try to build in such habits to their daily routine, he said. "Exercise buys you three to seven additional years of life. It is an anti-depressant, it improves cognitive function and there is now evidence that it may retard the onset of dementia," the cardiologist said. Cardiologists state that it is never too late to start exercising. Studies have found that people who start exercising at the age of seventy are less likely to develop atrial fibrillation, a heart rhythm disturbance that affects about ten percent of people over eighty.

According to Anne Procyk, Naturopathic Physician, one should have a goal of getting the heart rate up, simply to the point of being out of breath, when exercising, as that can lead to significant benefits.

The more active you are (and again it does not matter if you are older and starting your exercise program later in life), the more benefit you are going to have. Mild to moderate physical activity actually floods your body with natural healing "chemicals". Be careful not to overdo it though, as you do not want to overwhelm your body and create more inflammation. It is a well-established fact that regular mild to moderate exercise is one of the best habits you can adopt that will help you avoid depression, stay emotionally balanced, and improve your physical health. I do not think it usually matters what kind of mild to moderate exercise you do. What is important is to be active and use your joints and muscles regularly. Choose activities you enjoy and contribute to your wellbeing.

Stress-reducing exercises such as yoga, qigong, or tai chi can also be quite beneficial, as they are all great for easy stretches, deep breathing, relaxation, as well as restoring strength and endurance. Gentle stretching clears tension that builds when muscles tighten, improves overall circulation, and is relaxing. Proper stretching can reduce pain and stiffness. "Gentle yoga" is a mild approach to traditional yoga, making it an excellent option for those with limited flexibility or motion. The simple, functional, and repetitive moves can be done sitting in a chair or wheelchair, or standing using the back of a chair for support. Check with your local healthcare facilities to see what they may offer in regards to gentle exercise programs, or check online for "at home" techniques or programs if needed. There are also certain movements called micro-movements that one can do often. These have the ability to increase flexibility and banish aches and pains, therefore are worth researching.

If at all possible, I suggest walking every day with a positive, wise, and emotionally intelligent friend (if you do not have one yet, then seek to attract one). Walking by yourself in nature can also have enormous benefits to your overall health. Letting your gratitude list (or any other positive messages) repeatedly go through your mind while walking is highly beneficial! Getting outside and moving on a daily basis is uplifting for me. I even walk during the Illinois winter months. I bundle up, wear a face mask and boots when needed, and carry a hand warmer. No excuses here!

My mother-in-law gave me an awesome pedometer and it has made my walks even more interesting and fun! Pedometers can be great motivators getting you to walk more and all throughout the day. They can also be wirelessly connected to your computer to give you all sorts of fun data. Pedometers have been shown to increase physical activity in most cases.

A personal trainer or a health coach may help with your exercise or fitness goals. Just remember not to overdo it, especially if you are trying to restore your health. As always, be sure to check with your doctor before starting any exercise program.

- Also see the "Detoxify the Body" chapter for more on the benefits of exercise.

Chapter Eight

Get Grounded!

Grounding yourself (also called "earthing"), and allowing the positive energy of the earth to enter your body, can be extremely beneficial for overall health. Touching the ground gives us access to the earth's negative ion field, which is quite healing as it is emitting electrons all the time. Touch it with bare skin to absorb this powerful energy into your body.

It is quite easy to get grounded. One way is to simply place your bare feet directly on the ground (connecting with the earth). If you would like to make it even more powerful, you can spend some time mentally sending all negative thoughts, discordant energies, and "blockages to your healing" down into the earth, through your legs and feet. Then, after that, relax and visualize all the positive beneficial energy entering up and filling your entire body. Also, simply paying more attention to the earth beneath can help with this process. Any activity which connects us more to the earth, such as gardening, working with certain crystals and stones (such as Black Tourmaline), or just spending time outdoors (focusing on the natural world) can help as well. Countless people have reported improved health as a result.

Research has shown that spending just twenty minutes in nature can promote health and wellbeing. Try it and see for yourself!

"Grounding, or Earthing, uses the Earth's electrons like a magnetic mop, cleaning up positively-charged, inflammation-causing electrons and creating balance in your personal electrical circuitry. Simply put your bare feet on the ground and allow them up to soak up all of the good negatively-charged electrons. Studies have shown that standing on the earth for 20 minutes per day decreases cellular inflammation by 20%."

~ Christiane Northrup, M.D.

Chapter Nine

Sunlight

Getting some sunshine not only makes most people feel better, but it also helps reset the body's clock, improving sleep, and much more. You can refer to it at it as your "light therapy". Sit or stand in the sun and absorb the energy (and Vitamin D synthesis). Do this every day possible, and as tolerated (without overdoing it). The light from the sun enters your eyes and triggers your brain to release beneficial chemicals and hormones that improve mood, sleep, the aging process, and more. Use mindfulness techniques, involving all of your senses outdoors, staying in the present moment. Experience everything such as the warm sun on your face, beautiful nature views, the sky, the wind's energy, fresh air, and all wildlife. Enjoy and absorb!

"The sun is the supreme giver of all life and the greatest source of energy existing in our solar system. The receiving of sunlight not only works to

stimulate the brain, but is also held as one of the 5 essential elements in both Traditional Chinese Medicine and Ayurvedic Medicine. The field of epigenetics has further discovered that by simply exposing our naked skin to sunlight, over 3,000 epigenome DNA switches are turned on or off… the Vitamin D our bodies produce as a result of sunlight is maintained in our body's natural oils. Therefore technically, using soap within a 24-48 hour period after receiving sunlight can wash away these Vitamin D containing oils and prevent the Vitamin D from being absorbed into our bloodstreams. To protect yourself from sun over-exposure, I recommend consuming antioxidant rich foods prior to sun exposure such as green tea, berries, cacao beans and other antioxidant rich organic fruits, vegetables and herbs. If you have circumstances which require you to spend unusually long hours in the sun, or you burn easily, consider using a protective hat or seek out a natural organic sunscreen lotion; much safer alternatives to standard commercial sunscreens. Don't run from the sun, embrace it and activate a higher frequency of intelligence throughout your DNA today."

~ Joshua Eagle, Holistic Health Coach

- Along the lines of "light therapy", also see the "Other Non-Pharmaceutical Interventions" chapter for information on the therapeutic benefits of light boxes.

Chapter Ten

Therapeutic Massage

P rofessional massages can be another effective addition to your treatment plan. For health and wellness, therapeutic massage is an excellent way to relieve stress, reduce anxiety, improve circulation, induce sleep, reduce recovery time from exercise, and help the body heal. An increasing amount of research is confirming the health benefits of massage therapy for conditions such as fibromyalgia, pain, and so much more. The oxytocin system in the body stimulates painkilling endorphins during massage. Research suggests that it can boost serotonin by as much as thirty percent. Massage also decreases the stress hormone cortisol and raises dopamine levels. Because of all of this, massage improves sleep and reduces fatigue. An experienced massage therapist will also likely have knowledge of specific therapeutic essential oils which could be added to your therapy (as tolerated of course).

If you can find a massage therapist near you who is also an "intuitive", or one who is trained in multiple effective healing methods, those would be added bonuses!

I have seen a wonderful local massage therapist who does "relaxation massage" with me, but also adds "cranial sacral" which uses an intuitive energy healing approach. Using cranial sacral, diagnostics can be performed at the intuitive or energy level, and then certain massages and techniques can be done in order to get the body (and certain organs) "flowing" in the correct way. She also does Myofascial Release with me. Myofascial Release is a safe and effective hands-on technique that involves applying gentle sustained pressure into the Myofascial connective tissue restrictions in order to eliminate pain, restore motion, and much more.

This therapy is truly healing! I know this because I feel absolutely incredible during every appointment, and it has lasting effects. After each session, I also "pick her brain" for any and all insights, including "homework" she may recommend for me (which usually includes certain types of stretches which always feel great!). As a side note, no need to worry about "exposure" with professional massages as only one area is exposed at a time, with sheets over the rest of the body. You can feel free to keep on whatever clothing or undergarments you wish as well.

"Rejuvenate your body, mind, and spirit with a relaxing and healing massage. Special massage techniques reverse the negative effects of stress, repair damaged muscle tissue, and remove pain throughout your body. I use a range of massage techniques that improve circulation, detoxify your

body, relieve tension, improve digestion, enhance muscle tone, and increase mental alertness. Massages not only benefit the body, they benefit the mind as well".

~ Rita M. Vargas, LMT

Foot reflexology massages are another therapy to consider for your healing. These types of massages stimulate areas of the foot that correspond with certain organs and bodily systems. Some of the benefits of reflexology are said to include: easing tension and pain, improving circulation, and helping the body rid itself of toxins in a gentle way.

Acupressure (or meridian therapy) can be another beneficial healing activity, as it is used to treat a host of ailments and there is evidence of its success. It is an ancient Chinese technique that involves applying pressure to certain meridian points in order to provide relief, similar in principle to acupuncture. It addresses all aspects of a person as a whole, including body, mind, emotions, and spirit. It aids in relaxing muscular tension and boosts the flow of vital life force energy. Interestingly, it is possible to learn five of the most important acupressure points which one can utilize daily in order to ease tension and anxiety when they arise in the body and mind.

"Massage can benefit health in many ways. It can reduce heart rate, blood pressure and levels of stress hormone, enhance immune function, boost levels of endorphins and serotonin (the body's natural painkillers and mood regulators) and increase blood circulation - all this while easing sore and achy muscles. Massage certainly can help address the build up of lactic acid in muscles, and promote the clearing of normal byproducts of muscle metabolism..."

~ Dr. Andrew Weil

Chapter Eleven

Professional Psychotherapy and Hypnotherapy

Psychotherapy by a skilled therapist could be another beneficial add-on to your recovery program. Of course this is my specialty so I am a huge supporter of this mode of treatment! Insight-oriented, expressive, and cognitive behavioral therapy could all be quite helpful. If the therapist can add hypnosis or guided imagery, that would be a bonus! Mindfulness and energy psychology are also of great value in my opinion. EMDR (Eye Movement Desensitization and Reprocessing) is another effective therapy technique (especially with anxiety and post-traumatic stress).

- Also see the chapter "EMDR and Healing the Effects of Trauma" for more information.

There is also a hypnosis training program that exists which helps to provide relief from physical symptoms. The trained hypnotherapists work with autoimmune disease and more. I have a fascinating interview with the creator of that type of hypnotherapy which is located towards the end of this book. There is also another hypnosis provider, Rick Longstreth, out of Bloomington, Illinois, who does similar work (website: ahhh-hypnotherapy.com).

Fascinating results from a randomized controlled study, published in the Journal of Rheumatology (2013; 40:11), show that Internal Family Systems-based psychotherapeutic intervention had positive effects on patients with the autoimmune condition RA. The therapy decreased inflammatory markers, reduced pain and depressive symptoms, while improving physical function and self-compassion. The study was the first randomized control trial of its kind conducted to assess the efficacy of Internal Family Systems therapy on patient outcomes.

I urge you to look into what psychological treatment may be available for you. It is important to note that people who are depressed have elevated levels of stress hormones like cortisol, which can lead to medical issues. Chronic stress leads to inflammation, which is associated with every age-related disease, as well as countless other undesirable outcomes. If you have been feeling blue lately, check for these symptoms of depression: loss of pleasure or energy, change in sleep patterns or appetite, trouble concentrating, anxiety, guilt, irritability, sadness, or suicidal thoughts. If you have three or more of those symptoms, or if you have just one or two but have been feeling depressed for two weeks or more, it is time to get help (especially if you are having thoughts of hurting yourself).

For your growth, treatment, and healing I recommend seeing a mental health professional such as an LCSW (Licensed Clinical Social Worker), an LCPC (Licensed Clinical Professional Counselor), or a Clinical Psychologist. In-person psychotherapy is often covered by health insurance. There are also sliding-scale resources in most communities for those who cannot pay a full fee and do not have insurance coverage (or have poor coverage). At the time of this writing, there is an organization called Open Path Collective which connects clients in need with psychotherapists who have agreed to take some low-fee cases. Counseling and support over the internet and phone are now also widely available (iTherapy is currently an online counseling organization that can help you get linked up).

To find a therapist, you can also look online at profiles on listing websites such as PsychologyToday.com. There are also Employee Assistance Programs (EAP's) which you may have available if anyone in your family works for a corporation and has an EAP as one of the benefits. I work for a program where the client's corporation pays for what seems to be an unlimited amount of online video conference counseling sessions. Therefore, check your benefits to see if anything like that may be available to you.

I do encourage you to seek out and stay with a counselor who truly resonates with you. They are all a bit different and I suggest seeing a professional who will assist in reaching your highest potential and functioning (even at the physical level). I have heard stories where therapists have given certain messages to "chronic illness" clients such as "Yes you will be in pain for the rest of your life... Now let's work on acceptance and feelings of loss". Do not get me wrong, I know the importance of working through grief issues as well as any insight-oriented and expressive therapy that needs to take place, especially at the beginning of treatment. But I would not tell a client (or even mirror back) any message that reinforces something so negative that may never even take place in the future. None of us know what can happen with medical advancements, holistic health, spirituality, and more. Therefore I personally would not give any type of communication about such a pessimistic prediction. Not only do I find it unnecessary, but it can affect the outcome as well. When a client comes to a counselor, he or she can be vulnerable and highly receptive.

What is said in therapy has the potential to be received into the subconscious mind and therefore affect future behaviors. The "Law of Attraction" is also at play here, therefore be careful what is continually being discussed, accepted, and predicted, because more of the same will likely keep coming to you. Therefore, I think it is imperative to work with someone who can be a "cheerleader" of sorts, and assist you in a positive way, all throughout your holistic healing journey.

Chapter Twelve

Cognitive Behavioral Therapy

The Cognitive Behavioral Therapy (CBT) branch of psychology and psychotherapy focuses on how to help people prosper and lead happier, healthier lives, including functioning at a higher level. We can actually learn to be happy and have more energy by focusing on optimism, gratitude, and altruism. In cognitive therapy, the goal is to help clients identify and purge negative thinking patterns (or "distorted thinking") as a way to change how they feel. This approach has been quite successful and is strongly backed by research. Altering how we think about other people, our lives, our future, ourselves, and the world can produce powerful shifts. The ability to pull attention away from the chronic inner chatter of "lower" thoughts can be quite advantageous to health and well-being. You can begin by finding the silver lining in everything. When something that seems unfortunate happens, you can ask yourself, what could be a potential upside to this?

Negative thinking is one of the main contributors to chronic depression, and positive thinking is the most important aspect of CBT.

Surrounding yourself with material goods and a certain lifestyle may seem to lead to happiness, but how you really feel is mostly dependent on what is going on in your mind. When you choose to focus on positives, you actually help purge negative self-talk. This is important because persistent negative self-talk is one of the largest barriers to positive thinking. People become so accustomed to patterns of negative thinking that their minds pull them down automatically, even in situations where there appears to be nothing wrong. It can even be engrained within a family system as well, creating a "family history" of sorts. These people can become depressed, irritable, indecisive, anxious, and overly apologetic. Of course, then they also open the door to numerous stress-related physical conditions.

Here are a few common patterns or "cognitive distortions" seen with negative thinkers (if you recognize yourself in any of these, remember that acknowledgement is the first step in resolving the issue):

Filtering: This type of thinker will pull the negatives out of a situation and focus only on them, sometimes getting to the point of actually denying anything positive.

Personalizing: Some people seem to make everything about themselves. They will personalize all negative situations and assume that those things happen because they are unlucky, or as a result of something they did or did not do. They will often construct negative scenarios with "perfect" logic, providing reasons why everything is their fault, or set out to hurt them. They will also take things quite personally such as a friend cancelling an outing, when it might simply be due to illness or something else.

Catastrophizing: This involves anticipating and focusing on the absolute worst possible outcome. If something that seems unfavorable does happen, they will then use it to continue validating their negative "predictions".

Polarizing: This negative thinker sees everything as black or white only. A situation, person, thing, or the world is either perfect or it is awful. This type of thinking can affect every area of a person's life.

"Good thoughts bear good fruit, bad thoughts bear bad fruit."

~ James Allen

In study after study, CBT has been shown to be quite effective in treating depression. It gives sufferers the tools to stop downward spirals right when they begin and help them to see the positive aspects of themselves, their lives, others, and the world around them. It can also aid in ending the deeply engrained negative thinking patterns that are common in depression.

"Be careful how you are talking to yourself because you are listening."

~ Lisa Hayes

By practicing positive thinking, you can actually help prevent medical conditions while obtaining all the other benefits of having a positive outlook on life. Scientific studies have shown that there is a direct link between stress and the immune system. When a person is experiencing a period of stress and negativity, his or her body is less able to mount a strong and healthy response to bacteria and viruses, which tends to result in an increase in illnesses. Also, continually having a positive outlook equips people with tools to deal with serious health conditions. Approaching diagnoses such as cancer with optimism and self-belief has shown to have beneficial effects on healing as well as ability to tolerate treatments. Positive thinkers also have a lower incidence of cardiovascular disease and tend to have healthier blood pressure levels than those who do not engage in positive thinking. Optimists often have increased physical health as well as psychological well-being, and better skills for coping with stress and hardships.

CBT also provides helpful tools to assist in dealing with negative situations. Sometimes coping skills come down to refusing to give in to negativity and fears. For some, positive thinking comes quite naturally, but for others, outside assistance may be necessary to get on the right track and keep that going.

Studies conducted at the Mayo Clinic have confirmed the following health and well-being benefits of positive thinking:

- Increased life span
- Reduced risk of death from cardiovascular disease
- Greater resistance to the common cold
- Increased well-being (psychological and physical)
- Lower rates of depression and distress
- Better coping skills during stressful times

"Positivity presents an opportunity to step up to the next level of existence: to broaden your mind and build your best future."

~ Barbara Fredrickson

Let me give you another example of why thinking and feeling positive about the future is much better for your health and why it is the only option! Years ago, there was a situation where my husband told me he was going out of town for a week on a business trip. My usual reaction before this was to be overwhelmed by negative energy (pessimistic thoughts and feelings) and stress. I would say to myself "Great, I'll have to take care of the baby all alone", "It's going to be difficult", and so on. These types of thoughts and feelings create negative energy that runs throughout the entire body. I can always feel that when it is happening and it is toxic. Funny thing is this time the trip got canceled. So it was all for nothing! Now when he tells me about an upcoming trip, I vent a little, and then get working on setting up more childcare, activities, and anything else I need to do. I take it all one minute at a time, and do everything I can to think and feel optimistic. There have also been positive outcomes that have come from his trips, such as my son and I bonding like never before. Therefore, I do everything in my power to focus on positive scenarios and it provides me with more peace and joy. In addition, typically during the business trips we all do just fine, so there is no reason at all to let the toxic energy in. Think of all the situations you could apply this to in your life!

"Train your mind to see the good part in everything. See the goodness, the beauty, the kindness, the light, the love, and the joy."

~ Joyce Marter, LCPC

Learning simple techniques on how to live happily is just as important as any dietary or lifestyle change. Again, your thought patterns contribute in an enormous way to your overall state of health. Interestingly, acid levels in the body are also affected by thought patterns. According to the Mayo Clinic, stress affects many bodily systems, including heart function, digestion, blood pressure, reproductive function, oral health, cell growth and regeneration, as well as sleep. Put simply, thoughts create emotions and "negative" emotions produce chemical reactions in the body that can be highly acid forming. The good news is there are countless effective ways you can reduce the stress in your life and limit the effects of it on your body. This book is full of those recommendations. I encourage you to keep remembering that boosting your mental health is just as important to your body's functioning as your diet, and other lifestyle factors.

It can be beneficial to write in a journal until it all becomes second nature. Without judgment, write all of your negative thoughts down, let them go, and then re-frame them into positive thoughts. Lately I have been training myself to think and feel the affirmation "I feel good". I go through the day saying that to myself and it does wonders! When we continually think positive thoughts, the dopamine and serotonin levels in our brains change significantly. Just like our bodies respond to healthy nutrients, our brains respond to healthy thoughts. Give it a try and you will see!

"True health begins with your thoughts. Thinking about comfort, strength, flexibility, and youthfulness attracts those qualities into your life and body. Dwelling on illness, fear, disease, and pain does just the opposite. Your work is to notice and change your thoughts and move them in the direction of health and happiness."

~ **Dr. Christiane Northrup**

Chapter Thirteen

Solution-Focused Technique, "act as if"

There is a CBT technique called "Solution-Focused Brief Treatment". Simply stated, the theory is that if you continually "act as if" you already have the change you want, then that change will come to you.

Most importantly, life will improve the way you have desired. What you want out of life will be focused on, and not the problem. Many of you have heard of the "Self-Fulfilling Prophecy" and, simply stated, this follows that mindset. The "Law of Attraction" also closely works with "act as if" and affirms how powerful it can be in people's lives.

Solution-focused techniques can also improve relationship difficulties. What it has people do is change their behavior because, if there are problems, whatever they have been doing thus far is obviously not working well. For example, if your children consistently do not help clean up, and your "way" of trying to get them to do this is by yelling and criticizing, then is it clear that you need to change your approach. For example, you can try calmly and continuously saying statements like "We make the house nice together" (while really thinking, feeling, and acting as if that were indeed the case). Then see how that begins to change the energy and thus the dynamic. For another example, if you are trying to get others in your family to eat vegetables and you are feeling like a "nag" with no results, why not end what is not working and just start leading by example. "Act as if" everyone in your family is eating vegetables, provide them and continually make statements such as how you love eating them, how healthy you are becoming (or staying), and so on. See how that can transform things, as without that power struggle it will feel much different to all involved.

So, take something you would like to change in yourself or your life. Then ask "If that problem did not exist, what would I be doing differently?" Also ask "How would I be acting, thinking, and feeling that would be different?" Then act, think, and feel those new ways, give it some time, and see how your situation begins to change.

"A change in behavior, in most cases, will create a change in outcome. We often cling to behavior even when the results are not what we desire. We must be willing to change our actions if we want to change the outcome."

~ Justin Nutt, LSCSW, LCSW, LAC

There are a few precautions to take here in regards to "acting as if" with health issues, in my opinion. One is to make sure you still take care of yourself in all the ways you need for your particular health condition(s). Also, explain to those around you that even though it may seem like you are already well (as you will be "acting as if"), you will still need to spend quite of bit of time and energy focused on self-care and healing activities in order to restore your health. One last note along these lines is that I recommend that you plan for the worst, but then absolutely consistently expect the very best!

"Whether you think you can, or you think you can't—you're right."

~ Henry Ford

Chapter Fourteen

EMDR and Healing the Effects of Trauma

EMDR (Eye Movement Desensitization and Reprocessing) therapy is a remarkable, relatively new, natural treatment method used by EMDR-trained psychotherapists to heal the symptoms of past trauma, as well as other mental health conditions (and their effects on the body). It combines psychology and physiology in a way that allows a person to clear the negative impact of past traumatic experiences. These events can be as "minor" as a negative comment from a teacher, or as serious as a life-threatening incident. In any case, people are often unaware of how these past experiences are affecting their lives. It is interesting and important to note that in other cultures (such as Asian), it is fully accepted and understood that any kind of trauma affects the whole person. They understand that there is no dichotomy between the mind and body.

EMDR is definitely one of the quickest and most effective psychological techniques used to heal PTSD (Post Traumatic Stress Disorder).

It is backed by extensive scientific research and growing in popularity. The technique was developed by Dr. Francine Shapiro, a psychologist and educator. EMDR emphasizes disturbing memories as the cause of psychopathology and strives to alleviate the symptoms of PTSD. According to Dr. Shapiro, when a traumatic or disturbing life experience occurs, it may overwhelm normal coping mechanisms. Interestingly, Dr. Shapiro discovered the EMDR technique when she was personally experiencing disturbing thoughts and found that by moving her eyes back and forth, the memories dissipated. The theory is that trauma is the root cause of numerous conditions and if the trauma can be relieved, so can the resulting issues.

There is science behind PTSD symptoms and how traumatic experiences actually alter the brain. Emotionally charged events and associated messages tend to get filed by the brain under "important information" and therefore stored and recognized as vital data for keep for "survival". This is a way the mind protects us from "danger". If we are not aware, this data tends to run our lives in undesirable ways. The good news is that healing is possible! The effects of trauma can be reversed by reprogramming the mind and body.

Since an initial study in 1989, positive therapeutic results with EMDR have been continually reported with the following populations: those who have witnessed or been a victim of a disaster, clients suffering from PTSD, people who experience anxiety attacks and phobias, those who have suffered excessive losses, crime victims and first responders overcome with violent memories, and clients with chemical dependency concerns.

EMDR treatment applies bilateral stimulation, right to left eye movements (or tactile stimulation or sound), which activates the opposite sides of the brain releasing emotionally charged experiences stored in the nervous system. This action assists the neurophysiologic system, the base of the mind-body connection, to clear blockages and rewire itself.

This type of intervention allows clients to process serious concerns that they cannot yet talk about (but then can usually discuss freely after EMDR). More importantly, it can effectively eliminate unease surrounding the traumatic event, allowing new life into the once painful and distressing memory.

Simply speaking, during a typical EMDR treatment session, the therapist works with the client and asks him or her to recall all the memories around the traumatic moment or incident, evoking the specific feelings, thoughts, as well as physical sensations and experiences. During this time, the practitioner may hold his or her fingers about eighteen inches from the client's eyes and then begin to move them back and forth like a windshield wiper (although many use machines instead). The client follows as if intensely watching a ping pong game. The past experience is focused on, with the goal of it to fully come to "life" in session. As vibrant images arise, they are processed by the eye movements, and painful emotionally charged memories are replaced by tranquil resolved feelings.

Are you experiencing any of the following concerns?

- History of abuse of any kind (including abandonment or neglect)
- Continued anger, sadness, irritability, unpleasant thoughts and feelings, mood swings
- Difficulty making decisions, confusion
- Worry, fear, panic, hyper vigilance, obsessive thoughts
- Difficulty with trust
- Attraction to "unhealthy" people or things
- Feeling trapped in painful relationships or situations
- Self-blame, guilt, self-abuse, shame, self-consciousness

- Addiction

- Eating disorder

- Chronic physical pain

If you have answered "yes" to any of the above, you would likely benefit from EMDR. A therapist in my group practice is EMDR trained. She has seen countless clients with post-traumatic stress concerns, and has had much success with that form of treatment.

With EMDR, the client and the therapist become partners in helping to clear past traumatic blocked up energy. Arousal then decreases so the client can go back to a serene, grounded, and more content state of being. The goal is to help clients recover and let go of the past (understanding they are safe now), so they can have peace in their lives and function at a higher level. Again, we know this type of therapy will also likely help physical conditions due to the mind-body connection and the effects of chronic emotional stress on the body.

Brainspotting is a similar technique that has been shown to help people access, process, and overcome "negative" emotions, unwanted behavioral patterns, and even pain (including psychologically-induced physical pain). It utilizes bilateral sound and fixed eye placement to access subconscious trauma. It is relatively new and psychotherapists practicing this mind-body approach are finding it to be an effective treatment for a variety of mental health concerns. This fascinating method seems to activate the body's natural ability to heal itself from the effects of trauma.

On a related note, it has been discovered that an electrical forehead patch could also treat chronic PTSD. For the first time, a trial in a small group of patients recently showed that this new type of treatment for epilepsy and depression, that uses an external electrical brain stimulator, could also significantly reduce the severity of PTSD. NeuroSigma is licensing the technology and funding research. The company is already marketing the device overseas and plans to also make it available to patients in the United States.

Recently, I have also been learning that the simple act of coloring in a soothing, comforting, and supportive environment while recalling a traumatic or stressful event can have the same or similar positive healing effects on the brain as EMDR.

Chapter Fifteen

Emotional Freedom Techniques (EFT)

Emotional Freedom Techniques (EFT), also called "tapping", can assist as a valuable addition to your other treatments and activities. Studies are starting to prove its effectiveness. It has been used to facilitate the healing of the mind, body, and spirit. EFT has been known to help with a wide variety of concerns, such as anxiety, insomnia, pain, and even autoimmune diseases! It works with meridians, just like in acupuncture. I use EFT often and it has helped me tremendously. It is quite impressive how even the most basic tapping can calm (and refocus) the mind and body so effectively. Also, I love how it can be done without a practitioner when one has learned enough about it and the techniques. There are useful and easy video tutorials on the internet that will teach you the basics quite quickly. Just search "EFT" online and you will find loads of information. Currently, a trusted source is Nicolas Ortner and his website www.thetappingsolution.com. Nicolas has been one of the major practitioners behind the "tapping" movement. At the time of this writing, he has quite an active social media page that I highly recommend checking out as well: www.facebook.com/nortner.

"One of the questions I get most often is something to the effect of, 'Does tapping cure X?' where you can replace 'X' with cancer, fibromyalgia, IBS, and virtually any other disease you can think of. My standard is always this: Tapping itself doesn't 'cure' anything. Tapping – this emotional work, letting go, forgiving, stopping self criticism, clearing old traumas – HELPS the body heal. The body knows how to heal itself and when we get out of the way, it often does just that. One of the most challenging parts of any physical 'disease' is the emotional component, the stress, the self-criticism, and how they affect the body".

~ Nicolas Ortner

Chapter Sixteen

Spiritual Counseling, Guidance, and Education

Spiritual guidance and growth has been a must for my healing journey, and I continue to seek it wherever it exists. Without profound spirituality, it would definitely seem like a large piece of my "puzzle" was missing. For complex "chronic" conditions, any treatment plan that neglects the role of spirit is likely going to have limited effectiveness, in my opinion.

Along these lines, I have seen a spiritual counselor who helped me tremendously on my journey. She assisted me in seeing that I need to put myself first in every situation (except those involving my child, as I am his caretaker). This was a new and foreign way of thinking for me, but she made it possible to finally clearly see that it is not even beneficial to "save" people and they will end up just fine without me or my help. Tamping down my over-responsibility and letting people be resourceful on their own (and possibly even growing from their "difficulties") is actually closer to the way the world is supposed to work. From this different way of thinking, I have made some changes and better decisions in my life that I clearly see helps my health, physically, mentally, and spiritually.

"When you say 'Yes' to others, make sure you aren't saying 'No' to yourself."

~ Paulo Coelho

During difficult times, my spiritual counselor encouraged and taught me to ask my higher self, angels, God, or the Universe every day to show me what it is I need to know for today. This is especially helpful when experiencing some type of troubling symptom. I then ask what it is trying to tell me. I ask to be shown the message. She continually encourages me to stay in the "here and now" and be positive. She said I needed to have faith in the process that things are the way they are supposed to be, and everything happens for a purpose, even if I do not currently understand all of it just yet. Also, it is not God's plan for anyone to suffer. In addition, at any point, if you are feeling like you need a break from all the "lessons" in life, then ask for that break, and then do not block any efforts that the Universe is making in order to help you (for example: someone offers to babysit). Ask to be clearly shown all the "gifts" you have received from having certain difficulties. Ask to be shown right now. When I asked to be shown the "gift" I have received from experiencing autoimmune conditions, I was immediately shown that it was clearly LOVE.

"It is not the body but the mind that is in need of healing, and the only healing is a return to love... A healthy perception of our bodies is one in

which we surrender them to the Holy Spirit and ask that they be used as
instruments through which love is expressed into the world… The use of
the body for any other purpose than the extension of love is diseased
thinking."

~ Marianne Williamson

If you are open to it, you have an option of asking your "higher self"
questions such as: "What is the lesson and blessing in this situation? What are
the gifts?" Once we extract, process, and truly align with the lessons at a soul
level, while discovering and appreciating the gifts, we can stop repeating
unwanted patterns and begin to feel peace in our lives. "Higher self" (or
"higher intelligence") is associated with many belief systems, but the general
idea refers to an omnipotent, eternal, and infinitely wise being that transcends
our everyday consciousness. This is one's real self and intuition. It is that part
of you that connects directly to spiritual realms, or what some may refer to as
"Source". All of us are connected the divine, especially when we are open,
allowing, and work towards removing any blockages. This is the power that
most of the great geniuses and teachers of the past (and present) have accessed.
It can create magical and miraculous experiences in life.

Here are some suggestions if you would like to begin communicating
with your higher self:

Open your mind: For those of you who were raised with views that
neglected the "spirit", you may have to work on opening up your mind. To
establish close contact with spiritual realms, it helps to have your entire being

aligned with your goals. Also, be sure you are open to receiving information that expands your understanding of the higher self, the mind, the heavens, and the Universe.

Believe and expect: A necessary step is to simply believe that you have a higher self in which you can communicate. Then expect every day that this dialogue will occur and improve, as you focus on your growth. Therefore, establish a plan to communicate with your higher self, review that goal often, and be persistent.

Stillness and meditation: Arrange times to be completely alone and quiet. A peaceful place is best, with a goal of just doing nothing. This may feel strange at first but be patient. Give opportunity to hear your inner voice and it will occur either during that time, or later on. Something will happen (such as hearing a song saying exactly what you need to hear, or you will get a sudden spark of clear insight). All the great geniuses and teachers have found solitude for themselves, and you should as well. With meditation, you can discipline your mind and quiet down unnecessary thoughts. Create an opening for the higher self to fill up with wisdom that serves your highest good. For mediation you can concentrate on one thing such as a flame. Or visualize a light shining down and entering your dan tien area (just below the navel) filling your entire body with positive loving energy and healing light. There are countless practices to research and utilize. Using Aquamarine healing stones while meditating is said to help with increasing communication with the higher self.

"Wisdom grows in quiet places."

~ Austin O'Malley

Mindfulness: Focus more on the present, in the "now", as that is the only real moment anyway. While eating, be fully aware that you are eating, with all the tastes and aromas, and stay in the moment. While walking, just focus on your walking and all the sights and sounds. This helps in clearing the mind of everything such as worries and illusions. Once that anxiety we tend to accumulate is reduced, we are closer to our real selves, becoming more trusting and open to receiving wisdom and feelings of peace. Therefore, release from your mind that which no longer serves you, stay in the "now", and create quality space for your higher self.

Lessons: See life like a teacher. Whenever something happens, "positive" or "negative", ask yourself what the lesson is, and what the gift is. I believe even unpleasant people and situations can help us grow, transcend, and teach us what we need to know right now. Approach life as if the Universe is working to create your highest good! As you begin to view life as a scene in which you have the most powerful role, your higher self can become increasingly apparent in your life. Keep track of your discoveries, lessons learned, and gifts received!

Conversation: Have regular dialogue with your higher self, including statements such as: "I know you exist, and I am open to communicating with you and receiving guidance". This dialogue may seem one-way at first. Remember you have likely been out of touch for decades. It takes a while! On a long-term basis, persist like you are talking with a trusted friend or even a therapist (asking questions, openly expressing yourself, and sharing your hopes). Meanwhile, allowing answers to come.

Journaling: Regularly writing your insights, experiences, thoughts, feelings, and dreams in a journal will help you come into closer contact with your intuition. You can ask your higher self questions, and then later document the knowledge received. If you continually do this with openness and expectation, you will likely obtain the wisdom you are seeking. Journaling also helps us keep track of what truly matters in our lives.

Dream communication: Ask and expect your higher self to communicate in dreams. Before going to sleep, do some relaxation techniques. Then ask for guidance and clarity to come in dreams. Upon waking, recall and write in your journal. A potential issue you may have with the messages you are receiving from your higher self is that they can seem unclear or puzzling, especially if they come in dreams. It can help to write about the messages because sometimes answers become clear when journaling. Begin with how they made you feel and go from there. I also have asked my higher self specifically to give me more straightforward and direct messages in dreams and it has worked! If you are not used to remembering them, this will take time and persistence. However, with patience and openness, you will begin to recall your dreams, write them down, process, and receive answers.

Stay patient: Again, remember you may have spent your entire life out of touch with your higher self, and it takes time to re-connect. Keep practicing daily, and you will receive the knowledge you are seeking. If you begin to see repeated numbers (such as 333 or 11:11), or notice constant synchronicity occurring (above the realms of probability), these are likely communications affirming that you are on the right track. Keep thinking positively. You are shifting and entering into a new state of "self". Your consciousness is heightening and you are seeing the world for much more than what it seemed to be. Messages might come in unexpected ways. Be open, relax, and trust. Remember that the higher self wants to be in contact. The higher self is actually you. Therefore, communicate with the real you! Give it time.

"We are not human beings having a spiritual experience. We are spiritual beings having a human experience."

~ Pierre Teilhard de Chardin

It is absolutely necessary for me to add that watching and participating in videos recorded by Michael Golzmane can be quite powerful, and amazingly, at the time of this writing, many are free to watch online. His videos (and then subsequent services) have absolutely been the "icing on the cake" for my healing process, and coming across his information was "divine timing" for me. He is an experienced spiritual/energy healer and does "clearings" that are highly therapeutic in the deepest sense. If you have a chronic condition or issue, I strongly recommend viewing his information. If it resonates with you, consider obtaining individual and/or group clearings. Participating in this work has the potential to clear blockages and negative programs that are deep in the subconscious mind (sometimes completely outside of awareness), addressing the root causes of virtually all types of concerns. Michael has the ability to facilitate the resolution of complex chronic health conditions (including mental health and addictions), as well as severe relationship issues, career concerns, and financial woes. He does this by helping to clear the blockages and programs existing in the soul's history, meanwhile assisting one in more fully connecting with Spirit. Most of his work stems from what is called Spiritual Response Therapy (SRT). I would say that it leads people to feel much more hopeful and no longer feeling "doomed" down an unwanted path. His services work well for those that are open to it, and would be an excellent addition to any holistic counseling (preferably through a professional psychotherapist with a spiritual specialization). It would also be an outstanding healing activity to participate in during and after many suggestions in this book (like I said, it was the "icing on the cake" for me). Michael's website: www.clearandconnect.com.

If you have a serious issue such as a complex health condition and Michael's services have resonated with you but would like to take it a bit further, "Chris Kehler Holistic" is an option. Website: chriskehler.net. He is an Energy/Bio-Spiritual Healer. Just to be clear here, he has called himself "The Alternative to the Alternative"!

Also along the lines of spirituality, I would like to mention that we all have what is called an "aura" which represents our spiritual, physical, mental, and emotional energies. The aura is usually seen a blend of colored frequencies where each color expresses its own specific characteristics. Interestingly, special instruments are known to be able to detect it, and also to interpret the different colors and shapes which can reveal useful information. In scientific research it has been found that the aura is an electromagnetic field of energy that extends all around each one of us, for about four to five feet (in a healthy body) and appears to be depleted in "unhealthy" people. Along these lines, an individual is considered to be healthy in terms of physical vitality, mental sharpness, emotional wellbeing, and positive spiritual energies. A person who is high on all levels apparently will have a larger and brighter aura, and vice versa if unhealthy. Many healers claim to be able to see the aura of people. I recently had a hospital chaplain tell me I had an "aura of spirituality that was striking". Of course I was on cloud nine after hearing that! Apparently he was one of those people who could see auras.

Related to the idea of learning what we need to know here in this life, I had a colleague who is also a medical-intuitive and healer, Marilyn Nadulek, LCSW, tell me that my physical problems and symptoms had been serving to teach me life lessons (she also noted that everyone has a different reason for having medical problems, therefore that specific one does not apply to everyone). There were messages such as "leaky gut" issues stemming from self-criticism. She spoke about working with the "secondary" or "minor" chakras for joint health. Issues related to depletion of life force energy were also discussed, along with taking down any "walls" and allowing love from others.

In coming to an understanding of why we have a particular disease or symptom, at first, simply trust that there is meaning, perhaps many layers of meaning. Know that a disease frequently speaks to us on multiple levels all at once. Be careful not to grip onto only one explanation, excluding all others, especially with complex conditions. Just keep listening, opening up, and allowing, letting the messages of your body (and subconscious mind) take you deeper into self-understanding, growth, and learning, leading towards the completion of what I call your life's puzzle.

Also, related to the subject of spirituality, interestingly, during my illnesses, reading about near death experiences gave me hope, feelings of peace, and assisted in my healing process. Learning about these fascinating stories can dramatically change one's perspective on life. This quote from Anita Moorjani, the author of the book "Dying to Be Me" sums it up perfectly: *"It felt like I had become encompassed into some kind of universal energy, a completely limitless, timeless, all encompassing, magnificent energy. And it felt like this energy was both within me and outside me at the same time, and it also felt like the energy WAS me. It empowered me. I was given the choice of whether to come back or not, and immediately, I seemed to understand that because I now know how to allow this energy to flow through me, I was going to be healed."*

A few suggested "spiritual" books to read:

- "Dying to Be Me: My Journey from Cancer, to Near Death, to True Healing" by Anita Moorjani.
- "A Return to Love: Reflections on the Principles of 'A Course in Miracles' by Marianne Williamson.
- "The Power of Now: A Guide to Spiritual Enlightenment" by Eckhart Tolle.
- "A New Earth: Awakening Your Life's Purpose" by Eckhart Tolle.
- "You Can Heal Your Life" by Louise Hay.
- "The Dance: A Story of Love, Faith, and Survival" by Joan Aubele (Joan is a friend of mine).

A few themes running through most of the above books:

- We are all connected.
- God is inside all of us.
- We are here to love and feel joy, and experience the earth in our physical bodies.
- Stay in the "now", as the past and future do not really exist. Past and future are just illusions, and in other realms time does not exist at all.
- Physical illnesses can begin in the mind, and therefore many can be healed by the mind and spirit.
- Experiencing a high amount of fear can have significant health consequences.

- When we pass on, our spirits go into another realm, and just our true selves are still there. It is our core being that moves on and we are unconditionally loved.
- Heaven is not a location but refers to the inner realm of consciousness.
- Loving oneself is essential for health.

Being open and allowing things to come to you can offer the best life and the most meaningful accomplishments, instead of fighting against the Universe. Allow what is meant to be that supports your highest good, and it will just flow in, with positive energy.

"Have the courage to follow your heart and intuition. They somehow know what you truly want to become. Everything else is secondary."

~ Steve Jobs

My spiritual counselor also has continually stressed the importance of using "vision boards" for health, happiness, abundance, success, and so on. I highly recommend creating vision boards as well. It is a fun process and they work. I have seen it first-hand. You might as well get what you want out of life!

As far as additional spiritual services go, I had seen a shaman in the past, for several sessions. For the most part, I feel that Western medicine had failed me as far as treatment goes (diagnostically speaking, Western medicine helped at times, and just a few actual treatment plan recommendations have been beneficial to me). Therefore, if you are at all open to it and feel like something is missing in your diagnosis, treatment, or recovery (like in my case),

I suggest considering including a healer such as a highly qualified and experienced shaman. From these services, I received spiritual consultation, reiki-like treatment, energetic healing sessions, relaxation techniques, chakra balancing and education, crystal and stone healing instructions, "soul-retrieval", "cord-cutting", communication with spirit guides, intuitive readings, emotional support, and more.

Lastly, if you are at all connected with a church, consider utilizing any of the services during your path back to health. These organizations usually have people available who help folks pray or pray with them. Ask your church if there is anyone who can help you. There are also usually ways to request prayers for yourself and keep it confidential (if you want prayers but do not want it announced to the whole congregation). It may be possible to have consultations with a pastor or priest (or equivalent) as well, if that resonates with you. In addition, many churches have pools of money that have been donated for specific reasons. For example, if you know you need acupuncture, but have no current way to pay for it, ask your church if they have any resources available for people in need of treatment.

Chapter Seventeen

Support Groups

Another suggestion for your journey is to find a support group for your particular condition. When you come across one that resonates with you, speak with the leader and ask what activities and treatments specifically have been found to help those with the same condition. Also attending in-person support groups could be beneficial, asking the question to the group, "What has been found to be helpful for this condition or the specific symptoms that arise?"

With support groups, if there is a group member who seems to be much worse off than you, please do not fret. Remember that every case is different and it does not mean you are going down the exact same path. Take all the positive things you can get from the support organization. If there is something there that you do not believe will help you, in your mind just leave it there and do not bring it home with you.

There are online support groups on this website: mdjunction.com. It is an active online support group center, a place where people "meet" to discuss their feelings, questions and hopes, with like-minded people. You can join groups of interest to you. Asking your group members what activities have helped the most with their illnesses will get you heaps of information I am sure! Again, take all the positive things you can (and leave the rest there if you feel it will be unhelpful).

If you are having any feelings of shame over your condition or situation, support groups can help significantly. Connecting with others, being authentic, sharing, understanding, and feeling the sense of community all have the ability to diminish shame.

One more word of caution regarding support groups: A "woe is me" mindset on a long-term basis can be quite detrimental to health and wellbeing, in my opinion. Continuing on that path can stop people from functioning at their highest levels and receiving all that life has to offer. In a larger sense, this can be referred to as "victim consciousness". This is just something to keep in mind as some groups may gravitate towards this on a continual basis and I hope you find something more positive, inspiring, and healing.

Chapter Eighteen

Affirmations and Meditations

Meditating and using affirmations are powerful ways to begin reprogramming your mind, and assist in escaping the past and future (staying in the "now"). When you have a negative thought or negative energy, recognize it (without judgment) then you can use the following affirmations. Choose the ones which really speak to you. Keep repeating them throughout the day, and be sure to truly believe and feel them at the core of your being:

Healing Affirmations:

- Positive healing energy is flowing throughout my whole entire body
- I have the power and ability to accelerate my own healing
- My mind is powerful, and I now use it to heal myself
- I easily connect with, and surrender to, Source
- The energy from Universe enters my body and heals me
- I am 100% vibrantly healthy

- Perfect vibrant health is my divine right and I now manifest it
- My body is completely balanced, and every organ works beautifully
- Every cell in my body is healthy
- My body has been re-aligned and it works perfectly
- My body remembers how to be well
- I am grateful for all of my healing
- I deserve all healing and continually allow it to come to me
- I open myself up to all healing opportunities
- My health is completely restored, I am healthy, and I feel good
- Love is the answer and the cure
- Unconditional pure love is the most powerful healer
- Love flows throughout my entire body at all times
- I love myself deeply, completely, and unconditionally
- Love shines down from the heavens and I continually allow it in
- I am filled and surrounded by love and light from Source
- Love is all that matters
- Miracles happen
- I allow miracles to work and continue working in my life
- Good things happen to me and I allow them
- Abundance comes to me and I allow it
- My life is full of abundance and I have everything I want and need
- I am open to anything and everything that serves my highest good
- Nurturing myself is necessary for my healing and continued wellness
- I deserve nurturing from all positive sources, and allow it in
- Physical exercise floods my body with natural healing energy
- I take exceptional care of my body, mind, and spirit

- I am grateful beyond words
- I am grateful for every day that I am alive
- Tender loving kindness to everyone and everything, including myself
- I am forgiving everything in myself and others and feel totally free
- I regularly practice self-compassion
- The presence of God is everywhere
- God wants me to be happy, healthy, and loving
- I attract and keep positive healthy loving relationships
- I am kind to others and they are kind to me
- Others respect me, and I respect them
- I trust the process of life for myself and others
- I stand tall and I am equal to everyone else
- I am strong and powerful
- Life is getting easier and I am allowing that to happen
- I deserve total relaxation and leisure time
- I am safe

"Whatever you ask in prayer, believe that you have already received it,
and it will be yours."

~ Jesus (Mark 11:24; New Revised Standard Version)

Words which can create an abundance of positive healing energy:

- Love
- Joy
- Abundance
- Bliss
- Delight
- Wellbeing
- R-E-L-A-X
- Rejuvenate
- Refresh
- Illuminate
- Vibrant
- Energy
- Alive
- Peace
- Calm
- Tranquility
- Harmony
- Serenity
- Healthy
- Healing
- Euphoria
- Happiness
- Kindness
- Support
- Grateful

- Thankful
- Forgiveness
- Faith
- Angelic
- Positive
- Cheerful
- Nurturing
- Endorphins
- Leisure
- Divine
- Empower
- Infinite
- Hope
- Vitality
- Optimistic
- Fresh
- Humorous
- Smile
- Warmth
- Gentle
- Grace
- Inspiration
- Creativity
- Strength
- Success
- Wisdom

- Plentiful
- Invigorating
- Glorious
- Resilient
- Spectacular
- Celebration
- Wholeness
- Blessings
- Enthusiasm
- Nourishment
- Prosperity

Use all the affirmations and words which really speak to you (help you feel the healthiest, and ones you need the most). Working on your affirmations will get the positive energy flowing again! You will also naturally come up with more phrases on your own, after you begin going through your healing journey. Take notes from the books you are reading, jotting down any positive messages which really resonate with you. You will know which positive words and statements give the most healing energy (you will feel it in your body). Positive thoughts and feelings are quite powerful. Keep running these types of messages and thoughts through your mind as often as possible. Really feel them at your core. Emphasize certain words in your phrases (words you need the most at that given time). Even if the statement does not seem particularly "true" yet, "You might have to fake it till you make it", as my former acupuncturist used to say!

Put the affirmations on sticky notes, place them around the house, and stick them in other places where you will see them often. Say them into a mirror with a smile, including the statement "I love you deeply, completely, and unconditionally". Saying affirmations in the mirror to yourself looking into your own eyes will then allow the mind to more easily receive those messages and they will likely get instilled more deeply. Say it with passion. Write them down several times as that will make the affirmations even more effective. Seeing it on paper (and at all times throughout the day) also helps the integration into the subconscious mind. With affirmations and "feel good" words, why not go to a beach and write them in the sand? Or go there in your mind. What the eyes can see is an excellent reminder for the brain and heart as well! Countless successful people have used positive affirmations to get where they are today. Why not use it for your own life? It is free and easy! It does not even take much time because if you are ill, I am willing to bet your mind is full of negative thoughts all day, especially about the future. You can change them into positive affirmations and use those all day instead!

Affirmations are most effective when implemented into a daily routine. Your own quotes can be read, spoken, written, and thought about several times throughout each day. Repetition is an effective way to instill them deeper into your mind. The more you repeat them, the more you believe them, which in turn creates behavioral and life changes. Though the process may seem simple and silly if you are new to it, affirmations have the power to dramatically improve lives by helping to free people from their own negativity and self-doubt. Eventually, the more you work on your growth, positive thoughts transform your cognitive patterns and negative thoughts then become less prominent. The more you can recognize and release thoughts which no longer serve you, and consciously choose those that do serve you, the more your life will improve. Also important to remember is that the "Law of Attraction" is always at play and can create powerful positive changes in life as you move towards "upgrading" your mental programming.

"If you believe that you are a bad person, your cells are listening. If you believe that you are sick, your cells are listening. Likewise, if you believe that you are a beautiful being worthy of love and that you are healthy, your cells are listening. What kind of relationship do you think you are creating with yourself and your body if you're sending negative messages and embracing negative beliefs about yourself?"

~ Louise Hay

According to my spiritual counselor, all I need to say to myself (all anyone needs to say) is "I am deeply loved at all times". This is easy because there is absolutely no doubt it is true! Try it and see for yourself!

Keep in mind that the music we listen to often repeats in our minds, and like affirmations they can affect thoughts, feelings, and actions. Therefore, it is important also to choose your music wisely!

"Thoughts become things, choose the good ones."

~ Mike Dooley

Instead of complaining, ask for exactly what you want and need. Ask the Universe, healing angels, your spirit guides, God, Source, or whatever or whoever you feel positively connected with. Tell them what you want to happen (be specific) and exactly when you want it to occur (I usually say "now"). Meanwhile be sure to keep your receiving channels open and allow in the opportunities and changes that are coming your way.

"When you become intentional and on fire for what you want, the universe will deliver you every single thing that you've been wanting."

~ Lisa Nichols, Author

Find your inner joy, at your core, and really focus and meditate on that as much as possible. I can instantly access feelings of joy by focusing on my son, spending time with my little family, and hanging out with my favorite people. I am also able to access a considerable amount just thinking about this book and my writing activities. Some say that when you have joy, pain cannot exist at the same time. I have found that to be true as well. Give it a try. It will take some practice, but what have you got to lose? Nothing to lose and everything to gain!

Meditation is a proven stress reducer that helps instill a sense of calm and feelings of wellbeing. It can also clear the mind of any unnecessary negativity and connect you to what really matters in your life. While I suggest more than fifteen minutes daily if at all possible, even just a few minutes can have a powerful effect on your health and happiness.

A 2012 UCLA study demonstrated that participants who meditated reported significantly less feelings of loneliness as well as reduced blood markers for inflammation. In 2011, a study conducted by Wake Forest Baptist University found that meditation could reduce pain intensity by forty percent and pain unpleasantness by fifty seven percent. Morphine usually showed pain reduction at just twenty five percent. In 2010, researchers from Massachusetts

General Hospital showed that engaging in a mindfulness meditation program for eight weeks was linked to positive changes in the areas of the brain that relate to empathy, stress, and sense of self. In 2008, research conducted at Massachusetts General Hospital, in conjunction with Boston's Benson-Henry Institute for Mind Body Medicine, proved that meditation was a powerful method to lower blood pressure, even when pharmaceuticals could not. Almost sixty percent of patients in the study showed significant decreases in blood pressure levels and were able to reduce their medications. Along these lines, at my last doctor appointment, my blood pressure was the lowest it has been in twenty years! Therefore, my blood pressure level is now extremely healthy. Yes it is from all the lifestyle changes and healing activities I have been doing, but I am sure much of it is from meditative-type exercises. This is quite a success for me because it continually had been borderline high for so many years.

There are countless ways to meditate and not every method works equally well for everyone, as we are all a bit different. The Zen tradition of meditation has a great expression, "Invite your thoughts in but don't serve them tea." When sitting (meditating), you do not have to use energy in order to block out your random thoughts, however, do not engage with them either. Just learn to let them simply drift away. Thoughts sometimes arise during meditation, no matter how experienced one is. The key difference between the novice and the experienced is how much those thoughts are able to interfere with one's clarity, peacefulness, self-love, and connection to the divine.

The way I do my formal meditation is in a similar position as acupuncture, therefore it is usually in a recliner. You can also mediate in the traditional position, whatever works for you. Always "meditate" on positive messages at any time you possibly can throughout the day (such as on your daily walks, during tasks, and while you are lying in bed). During meditation, you can imagine floating up in the air envisioning a white light shining onto you. Then "allowing" in pure love, creating a wonderful feeling of peace and connection, which nothing can disrupt.

"Today, perhaps more than ever, illness of the body is rooted in the functioning of the mind. We are anxious, pent up and frustrated, and our emotions are making us sick. There are however natural remedies to living a happier and healthier existence without needing to rely on psycho-pharmacopeia. One of the most powerful solutions is meditation..."

~ Adam Cantor, MS, Lac

Chapter Nineteen

"I Am Safe"

D uring your journey back to health, an essential positive affirmation to utilize is "I am safe", as an underlying long-term feeling of being unsafe is linked to certain diseases, particularly autoimmune conditions. One of the leading stress and trauma researchers is Dr. Stephen Porges out of the University of Illinois. During his work on understanding the nervous system, Dr. Porges discusses "the metaphor of safety". Interestingly, he has vigilantly recorded how chronic patterns of feeling unsafe are linked to immune system conditions (such as fibromyalgia). I have also read that many respected Emotional Freedom Technique (EFT) practitioners have recognized the link between ongoing concerns about safety and severe immune system problems.

Therefore, working on changing one's worldview, as well as continually including affirmations such as "I am safe", will likely help with autoimmune and other chronic complex conditions. Instead of seeing the world as something that is always assaulting, look at how you can have fun, allow in love and positivity, help others, and trust the path of life. Also know you can actually have faith in yourself to be there for the all-important role of self-care. There are countless additional suggestions contained throughout this book that have the ability to significantly increase one's feelings of safety and security.

Along these lines, here is a highly beneficial affirmation to use on a continual basis, originating from the work of Louise Hay: *"I relax completely for I now know I am safe. I trust Life and I trust myself."*

Chapter Twenty

Loving Yourself

The act of loving yourself is absolutely one of the most important activities you can do for your health and happiness. When you truly love yourself everything in life seems to fall into place. You find fulfilling work, you are attracted to people and situations that support you highest good, you eat nutritious food, you take care of your body, and easily receive from all positive sources. Repeatedly using affirmations such as "I completely love myself unconditionally at all times" is one activity you can do to create more self-love.

"Love yourself like your life depends on it, because it does."

~ Anita Moorjani

Here's a basic introduction to Louise Hay's therapeutic exercise called "mirror work":

"While looking at yourself in the mirror affirm the following: I love you _____ (insert your own name). I really, really love you. You are my best friend, and I enjoy living my life with you. Experiences come and go; however, my love for you is constant. We have a good life together, and it will only get better and better. We have many wonderful adventures ahead of us, and a life filled with love and joy. All the love in our lives begins with us. I love you, I really love you."

So, take a deep breath and just say "I love you, (your name), I really, really, love you" every time you pass by a mirror, along with a big smile. This will instantly start increasing your self-love. I say it to myself like I say it to my son!

"Please encourage people to be very kind to themselves when they do this practice. I know that mirror work can be very confronting at first. It reveals your most basic fear and your most terrible self-judgments. But if you keep looking in the mirror, you will begin to see through those judgments and see who you really are. Your attitude to mirror work is the key to success. It's important to take it lightly and be playful. If it helps, I prefer that people stop calling it mirror work and instead call it mirror play."

~ Louise Hay

Why not give yourself a hug? You can wrap your arms around yourself and give a huge hug (including a big smile)! Also resolving any guilt feelings will help increase feelings of self-love. In addition, nurturing the self is necessary. Some people have deep subconscious beliefs that they do not deserve to be healthy, are unworthy of love, or cannot (or should not) receive nurturing. Maybe there are some guilt feelings, low self-worth, or resentments. Many people are not even aware of these "programs" that are actually running their lives. It is important to pinpoint those feelings, and the messages you are giving to yourself. Take some time to identify and release them (future chapters have suggestions for doing so), and make sure you often use affirmations such as "I deserve good health", and really feel that to your core.

Other ways to show self-love are in actual self-nurturing actions. One example can perhaps include your skin lotion, applying it slowly like in caressing motions (showing love and nurturing). We can also think or say that we love each part of our bodies as we lovingly touch them (such as "I love my hands"). Try it for a while and see what transpires!

"Spiritual malady manifests as the false beliefs in unworthiness, emptiness, fear, shame, not enoughness and so forth. We become addicted which simply means becoming enslaved or in bondage to those erroneous ways of identifying ourselves."

~ Ester Nicholson

Most of us know how it feels when first falling in love with another person and the euphoric feeling that often occurs. How about if we had "love affairs" with ourselves? Well, you can fall in love with yourself the very same way. As time goes on keep rekindling that love affair as well!

Again, my spiritual counselor recommends putting myself first in every decision I make (except when it comes to my son as he is dependent on me). Putting yourself first with important decisions is another way of following it up with actions and actually showing self-love.

"You and your life are sacred. It is your primary responsibility to care for yourself with great love. When you do this, your capacity for loving and caring for others will be strengthened, not diminished."

~ Joyce Marter, LCPC

Why not write letters to yourself as if writing to a loved one? Be sure to include encouragement of self-nurturing and make sure you are not judging yourself negatively. Tell yourself you are a remarkable person and add a reminder that you are always deeply loved. This practice can transform your life! You can also leave love notes and reminders on sticky notes, place them onto your dashboard and desk areas, type them into the "notes" section of your phone, and write a special reminder word right into your calendar! If you cannot think of something positive about yourself at first, do a trade with someone else and write notes for each other to use. I assure you this will soon become second nature and will be instilled in your mind in no time!

"When people start to love themselves more each day, it's amazing how their lives get better. They feel better. They get the jobs they want. They have the money they need. Their relationships either improve, or the negative ones dissolve and new ones begin."

~ Louise Hay

With guilt feelings, a good question to ask yourself is whether, knowing what you know now, you would still commit the act. If the answer is "no", then you have learned your lesson and it is time to completely forgive yourself and move on. If it was an especially difficult situation or decision and you still would have done the same thing now, then you need to let go of the guilt, forgive yourself and know you did the best you could, given the situation. Further "punishing" yourself is not at all productive and can cause further damage. Take some time to fully forgive, release, love yourself, let go, and move on with a healthy positive life.

Rose Quartz is a healing stone you can carry with you which can help increase all types of love! These stones have a wonderful "loving vibration" and assist in increasing feelings of wellbeing. I have also personally found that they are great to use during periods of grief and loss when your heart aches.

- Also see the chapter "Balancing the Chakras; Using Healing Crystals and Stones" for more information.

If you consistently have been an extremely negative person who criticizes yourself and others, and sees life through pessimistic and limiting eyes, then it is going to take some time for you to transform that way of being and to become positive and loving on an ongoing basis. I do not want you to get angry because you are not doing it quickly enough. Please be patient and gentle with yourself as it takes time.

"Life is too short, hug a little longer, love a little stronger, forgive a little sooner and smile a little sweeter."

~ Caroline Naoroji

Chapter Twenty-One

Loving Others

Loving yourself is a key component in truly loving others. Sending out love daily is also necessary, and then more love comes back to you. When it comes to you, it must be allowed in, and only you can do that.

"Love is too enormous to be contained. It's too valuable to be owned and too dynamic to be reduced to words or symbols. This is why love, manifested through actions, will be the elixir that unites our fractured, chaotic and terrified world."

~ Paul Hokemeyer, LMFT

If you are finding it difficult to send out love, in addition to working on self-love and allowing love in, I recommend doing the following affirmation every day: "Loving kindness to everyone and everything". Also "I love (add name) with all my heart", meanwhile imagining sending love to that other person with both hearts glowing and connected with pure unconditional love.

"How do we love others? Accept them as they are. Allow them to be themselves. Stop trying to change them. Let them take care of their own growth processes. We can't learn for another. If their behavior is detrimental to us, then we may choose not to be in their presence—and that is fine. We must love ourselves enough not to be brought down by self-destructive people. If we have many negative people in our lives, then we can look to see what pattern there is in us that attracts these people to us."

~ Louise Hay

Surrounding yourself with positive "higher vibration" people is important. Healthy social supports can be great stress buffers, and authentic connections can be healing.

When you find yourself around negativity, however, see yourself as rising above it, and keep the positive thoughts and feelings continually running throughout your mind and body. Be careful not to "absorb" the negative energy, and keep the connection with any negativity or toxic people as brief as possible (especially while you are healing). Strive to resolve any guilt feelings you may have about this. Always make it known that "bad vibes" do not have a "home" with you. This can also be possible with strong self-love and the powerful act of bringing loving energy to any situation or conversation.

"You cannot hang out with negative people and expect to have a positive life."

~ Joel Osteen

It is important to note that assertiveness training is quite effective for certain conditions, such as social anxiety, relationship issues, low self-respect, and problems resulting from unexpressed anger (such as depression). If you find yourself being too passive, passive-aggressive, or overly aggressive with others, then it is highly likely you would benefit from this type of intervention. Working with a therapist or doing some online studying on the subject of assertiveness training will likely help your relationships and overall wellbeing.

Remember that people with active autoimmune conditions have the potential to be overly sensitive and therefore have to be careful not to "absorb" negative energy. They frequently process the environment in a deep way that easily over-arouses them, affecting many aspects of their lives. They can usually sense negative energy before others do. This has some benefits but it also can have consequences. If this sounds like you, be aware that the negative aspects of this can dissipate as you work on your growth and healing. Meanwhile before going into a situation that might not be good for you, imagine a bubble around yourself before going there. This bubble will give added protection so that you do not absorb anything "harmful", and can keep the positivity and health flowing inside you. This bubble can be any color you wish, whatever gives you the most comfort and feeling of protection. It can also be helpful to keep repeating affirmations such as "I am strong and powerful" and "I only allow in that which serves my highest good".

- Also see the information on the "protective" nature of Black Tourmaline stones in the chapter "Balancing the Chakras; Using Healing Crystals and Stones".

"People don't always handle situations the way we'd like them to. The neighbor I considered a friend must have found my travails too difficult to bear and ignored me. But the neighbor who wasn't a close friend, rose to the occasion, and cared for the girls on weekends, and found some time to take Theresa and Allison to shop for school supplies and their new fall wardrobes. It's fortunate that the good outweighs the bad in this world."

~ Joan Aubele, Author of "The Dance: A Story of Love, Faith, and Survival"

Obviously people do not always think before speaking or acting. They occasionally say and do things that can be quite hurtful. Sometimes, unfortunately, it might be intentional, but other times completely unintentional or it is simply due to carelessness or ignorance. But always remember that your mind can be trained to see the good in everyone and everything. People are imperfect beings. When we learn more about spiritual teachings, we are guided into love that comes from the heavens, the pure love that heals us all. Perfection is in spiritual realms. I believe that prior to our experiences on earth, we are "perfect" spiritual beings. This is before life has a chance to shape our egos. Deep down inside each and every one of us is a spirit that is pure, good, vibrant, and full of unconditional love and happiness.

"Not all wounds are so obvious. Walk gently in the lives of others."

~ Author Unknown

Take an honest look inward and increase insight to see what you are doing or not doing that is helping or not helping in this area of your life (with other people and relationships), and also remember the following quote:

"You can't expect to draw people into your life who are kind, confident, and generous if you're thinking and acting in cruel, weak, and selfish ways. You must be what it is that you're seeking—that is, you need to put forth what you want to attract."

~ Dr. Wayne W. Dyer

It is essential to let go of judgments and blame. Live more in the moment and work on releasing any blame or judgments from your thoughts and comments. Catch yourself, and give it some consideration, when you find you are blaming or judging, or using past history as a reason for your current actions (or non-action). Be careful not to fall into "victim consciousness" as it can be quite detrimental. Take charge of your life! You are strong and powerful! You can have the things and experiences that you desire in life!

"When you point your fingers at someone, look where the other three

fingers are pointing".

~ Twylah Nitsch

I have also found that if you treat yourself the way you want others to treat you, then you are not only getting the benefits of self-love, but others will notice and often follow in their treatments of you.

Along the lines of other people and relationships (and adding the all-important authenticity piece), I just love the following quote:

"Just be yourself. Let people see the real, imperfect, flawed, quirky, weird,

beautiful, magical person that you are."

~ Mandy Hale

Because we are all connected, always remember this quote from Princess Diana: *"Carry out a random act of kindness, with no expectation of reward, safe in the knowledge that one day someone might do the same for you".*

If you seem keep finding yourself in the middle of unnecessary negativity and drama, it will be helpful to use the following positive affirmation (from John Assaraf) on a daily basis:

"My life is FREE from negativity and drama. I surround myself with LIGHT and LOVE."

Also along the lines of loving others, it is important to note that positive relationships and touch are essential for your brain's feeling of happiness. Surprisingly, one way to release oxytocin is through touching (oxytocin is a neurotransmitter and a beneficial hormone). Touch is something we can do here in the physical world that we cannot do in spiritual realms, so by all means take advantage of it while you are here! Obviously, it is not always appropriate to touch people, but small gestures like handshakes and pats on the back are usually fine. In social and occupational realms, touching can make you more persuasive, increase team performance, and much more! For people you are close with, it can be beneficial to lovingly touch more often.

As far as health goes, touching someone you love can actually reduce physical pain. Interestingly, studies have been done on married couples and actually the stronger the marriage, the more powerful the effect. In addition, holding hands with someone you love and trust during painful situations can help comfort you as well as your brain.

Therefore, be sure to spend time with people you care about and include hugs whenever possible. Neuroscientists have recommended long hugs as they tend to release more oxytocin. Research has shown getting five hugs a day for four weeks significantly increases happiness. If you do not have anyone for "touch" right now, neuroscience research has suggested obtaining professional services from a licensed massage therapist.

Many additional ideas throughout this book can aid in improving relationships (including content in the following chapter). One additional specific recommendation is to make a gratitude list about someone in which you seem to be having trouble. Write everything you appreciate about him or her and keep referring back to the list as much as possible. You can even tell the person what you are grateful for and then see the energy and dynamic start to shift.

Chapter Twenty-Two

Identifying, Expressing, and Releasing Emotions

Dealing effectively with your emotions will help reduce stress on your mind and body, and therefore will likely increase overall health. Sometimes there will be emotions which pop up that need to be processed. They may be deep-seated from long ago or just a few hours ago! Nonetheless, it may be necessary to express and deal with them in order for your health to continue to improve. If you are feeling down, depressed, irritable, anxious, or unhealthy, it is likely a sign that some feelings (conscious or subconscious) need attention.

You may have experienced traumatic abuse of some kind, perhaps during your childhood. It could have been physical, verbal, emotional, sexual, or even abandonment. It is important to note that it does not need to be life-threatening to be reappearing in your life as a repeated energetic cycle. The earliest event as well as subsequent experiences could have made you feel like you deserve abuse and are unworthy of respect. As a result, you may have diminished self-esteem and self-respect. Your boundaries were not acknowledged and most likely you were consciously or subconsciously made to feel negative about yourself, others, and the world. Sensitive people will have had the most difficult time with these situations, as typically they grow up like little "sponges" soaking up everything in the world around them. One example might be, from professional experience, I have seen that growing up in a judgmental family system contributes to social anxiety, including frequent thoughts such as "The whole world is judging me". When looking at autoimmune cases in particular, where an individual's body seems to be working against itself, there can be a subconscious feeling of deserving to be hurt or abused, maybe even hatred of self. In addition, many times there is a deep sense of unworthiness to be healthy. Recognizing negative patterns is the first step in healing. Many recommendations in this book will help to remedy this as well (including specific therapeutic activities and affirmations). It is a good idea to say affirmations to yourself (and really feel them at your core) over and over all day every day until you feel like they are completely engrained into your mind and body. Affirmations such as: "I deserve all nurturing from all positive sources", "I deserve to be vibrantly healthy", and "Good things come to me and I allow them", along with actions of self-love, will be extremely helpful.

There is growing evidence that psychological distress during childhood leads to increased risk of medical problems later in life (stress in childhood influences adult health). This suggests that it could be counter-productive to educate patients on life style changes without addressing the underlying distress that may be fueling unhealthy behaviors. With autoimmune and other disease conditions, we know that often the physical symptoms are accompanied by past emotional trauma. It is known that when you work on the body, mind, and spirit, the benefits to overall health increase significantly. Some even say that trauma is the root cause of most chronic illness (such as autoimmune conditions).

There is a book out that covers this very issue entitled "The Deepest Well: Healing the Long-Term Effects of Childhood Adversity" by Nadine Burke Harris, M.D. It contains absolutely fascinating and essential information. This physician reveals how childhood stress leads to lifelong health problems and what can be done to break the cycle.

"You are not a helpless victim of your own thoughts, but rather a master of your mind. What do you need to let go of? Take a deep breath, relax, and say to yourself, "I am willing to let go. I release. I let go. I release all tension. I release all fear. I release all anger. I release all guilt. I release all sadness. I let go of all old limitations. I let go, and I am at peace. I am at peace with myself. I am at peace with the process of life. I am safe."

~ Louise Hay

In a loving and non-judgmental way, identify what you are feeling. One of the best methods I can suggest in order to increase insight and express your emotions is journal writing. The rules are simple: no censorship, no one else being able to read it, just pure flowing thoughts and feelings onto paper. If your heart could speak, what would it say? Regular journal writing in this manner can be extremely beneficial to your health.

Identifying and clearing out anger, along with other emotions, will free you to experience a more peaceful and fulfilling life. One method you can use to help in this process is what some in the therapeutic community are now referring to as (excuse the language) "The Shitty First Draft" (SFD) technique which I learned from a recent seminar given by Lisa Pisha, MS, LMFT, CDWF:

"The first draft is the child's draft, where you let it all pour out and then let it romp all over the place, knowing that no one is going to see it and that you can shape it later. You just let this childlike part of you channel whatever voices and visions come through and onto the page. If one of the characters wants to say, 'Well, so what, Mr. Poopy Pants?', you let her. No one is going to see it."

~ Anne Lamott

Utilize the SFD writing technique with any scenario that seems to provoke reactions in you. If you feel like you are "over-reacting" to a certain situation (like it is really getting "under your skin"), then it is exactly about which you should be writing a SFD. I am talking about emotional as well as physical symptoms (such as heart racing or GI discomfort).

The following prompts can help be your guide:
- The first thing I want to do
- My emotions
- My body
- My thinking
- My beliefs
- My actions

After you have gotten all of it onto paper you will likely feel a release as well as increase in your insight (deeper knowledge of self). This leads to not only discovering some root causes of your triggers, but it dissipates their negative effects on your mind, body, relationships, and life. Seeing them on paper helps the writer to get them out into the open and understand they are not so scary after all. Then the mind and body do not have to spend energy continuing to stuff them down when provoked. This leads to reactions becoming less and less especially when more of this technique is used.

A second draft then gives the person a chance to re-write his or her story. This activity continues the therapeutic process.

I have seen firsthand that the SFD activity helps to heal the mind from what is currently being termed as "trauma brain" by many of my colleagues. As a result of these types of activities, you can achieve a more relaxed and balanced mind-body condition, allowing you to take back your power and no longer having old wounds running your life!

There are some additional healthy ways to identify and express feelings when they arise. These include: talking to someone you trust, watching "tear-jerking" movies, listening to music that you know will evoke feelings, or pounding on a pillow while releasing emotions. Some people also go for power walks and imagine what they are upset with is under their feet and they are stepping on it, or the person, all the way. Meditating in a quiet comfortable place focusing on your heart area is another option. Acupuncture has a way of helping to release emotions as well, sometimes resulting in some tears. There are also more specific acupuncture treatments that pinpoint the main goal of emotional release, such as in cases where there is a history of trauma. Reiki sessions can also draw out emotions in a quite profoundly therapeutic way, providing a much-needed release. Crying while in the shower is also an option, in order to release feelings in a comfortable place and in private (particularly useful if you tend to have small children around watching and asking questions about everything that is happening!). Walking outside at night is also a private way to identify and clear out emotions as no one will be able to see the tears.

Working with specific healing crystals and stones is another option to help identify and let go of repressed emotions and memories. In addition, again, if you are open to it, communicating with your "higher self" can be a therapeutic way to process feelings.

- Also see the chapter "Spiritual Counseling, Guidance, and Education" for more information on dialogue with your higher self.

If you think that there is something you may be feeling guilty about, one idea is to determine what can be done to make it better for that person (or situation) that you feel you may have "harmed". If it is something from long ago and there is not much you can do about it now, then simply keep telling yourself statements like "I forgive myself" and make sure to include these statements in your list of specific affirmations to use. Imagine saying you are so very sorry, why, and how you feel, while releasing the emotion. Follow it up with "I forgive myself for everything". Deep complex guilt may need a bit of "divine intervention" to pinpoint, process, and let go. There are also other activities which can help with guilt feelings, such as donating to a specific related charity or helping someone in need which may remind you of something you may feel guilty about from long ago. All of this can help you heal. Just remember that forgiving yourself will be extremely important to how you treat yourself, what thoughts you have, and ultimately to your healing process. You will need all the self-love you can get!

If you find that you are having trouble identifying and releasing deep "negative" emotions, resentments, or guilt, ask for more help. Again, sometimes these types of things need a bit of "divine intervention". If so, ask the Universe, the heavens, God, angels from God, healing angels, Jesus, or what some call "Source" to help you identify and release anything that might be getting in the way of your healing (past hurts, old wounds, resentments, shame, and guilt feelings). Also, if you are having difficulty with any of the affirmations or activities, this may indicate an old wound, guilt/shame, or resentment in need of attention. If you feel any need for professional assistance then by all means go ahead and get it, from a treatment provider or healer who resonates with you.

Imagine that you are releasing these lower emotions into the heavens (the divine is non-judgmental and all-understanding). You can do this while deep breathing (during the exhale). You could also release them down into the earth (while sitting or standing with your bare feet on the ground). In addition, some use crystals such as Rose Quartz in hand and imagine them releasing into the stone (these crystals are "absorbent"). In the shower you can also use the affirmation "Let the water carry away that which no longer serves me".

Releasing the blockages and the darkness will open you up to fully receive the love and the light. This is true healing. Make it known that you strongly desire to have all of the past emotional pain and wounds be cleared from your body and mind. Make it known that you are not afraid to have all of that past negativity be removed. Then continue to "act as if" it has all been released. The Universe will then act on your request and past emotional pain will be alleviated in various ways. It will either just start to happen, or you will be presented specific therapeutic activities. Pay attention and act on those opportunities which resonate with you. You will then likely feel lighter. Ask that all blockages be opened and make it clear that you want to be filled with love. Then "act as if" the blockages have already been released and you are already filled with love (and are open to receiving even more goodness). Then you need to purposefully allow in the unconditional love from every source possible. After some practice this will all become second nature, and like I said it is truly healing!

After expressing and releasing your deepest feelings and emotions, be sure to pat yourself on the back and reward yourself. Immediately begin thinking nurturing and caring thoughts towards yourself and even speak them aloud. Having a mirror in front of you will help instill this even deeper, and be sure to give yourself a big smile. Then have a plan for doing your favorite activities. For example, I might curl up on the couch, watch a good movie, and drink a cup of chamomile tea. So, do whatever feels nurturing and healing for you. If you can then tell your story in a heartfelt genuine way and it does not make you feel like crying, healing has occurred. Along the way, always remind yourself of all the positive things you do have!

"I am free now to detach myself from what used to be."

~ Dr. Wayne W. Dyer

Chapter Twenty-Three

Give Yourself Permission to Feel "Down" at Times

Sometimes you will just have to give yourself permission and accept the fact that you are feeling "down", sad, depressed, fearful, annoyed, and/or angry, with no judgement. Life throws all of us some extremely difficult situations. There have been times when EFT tapping did not work the "usual" way for me, like after my father passed away. Doing EFT techniques shortly after he died just made me cry (but was probably a needed release for me). Also, sometimes it is likely you will not be able to sleep well because of something you are dealing with that is extremely stressful and upsetting. It is ok, and you have to fully accept and allow yourself to feel and be a certain way. You know it is only temporary and that you will get back to all your usual positive affirmations (and other healing activities) as soon as you feel you can do them again. Remember that excellent self-care during these times is imperative! Affirmations such as "I love myself", and "Everything is exactly the way it is supposed to be right now even if I do not yet understand it" are going to be important to keep saying ongoing, all throughout these tough times.

"Feel what you feel and allow it to pass. Don't judge your feelings or yourself for having them. Do not label your feelings good or bad, right or wrong. Drop your hands to your sides and give yourself permission to ride out the emotional tidal waves that are sure to surface every now and then. Each time an emotion surfaces, this is a sure sign that you are working through it in order to release it."

~ Iyanla Vanzant

Chapter Twenty-Four

Releasing What is Bogging You Down

A long the lines of clearing old emotions, resentments, hurts, and wounds, it is beneficial to let go of actual items you no longer need. It can help you feel lighter. Take your time with this because you do not want to overwhelm yourself. At your own pace, begin going through all of your belongings and put each item into a category. My categories have included:

- Keep and use
- Keep and store away
- Put out to curb with "FREE" sign
- Sell at re-sale shop on consignment
- Donate
- Recycle
- Discard

There are countless benefits to freeing yourself from items which no longer serve you. Again, you will likely feel lighter. In addition, you can donate to a place which helps people (others who need your items will actually be using them right away, and charities can benefit from the sale money). The Universe usually returns the favor so be ready to receive (and allow) some goodness for yourself after giving to others. You will have open space for even more to come your way. Clearing out the extra items can also make your home seem cleaner and larger. In addition, the benefits include actually finding belongings you had forgotten about or that you thought were lost and gone forever! Making extra money selling your items is another potential bonus, and donations can be tax deductible!

Always remember: YOU DESERVE TO LIVE IN A BEAUTIFUL SPACE. Keep telling yourself that repeatedly until it gets deeply rooted into your subconscious mind and the desired changes are occurring.

"Piles of stuff in our homes are one of the greatest stress triggers. Clutter literally increases your cortisol level! When we have a lot of clutter in our homes, it has the effect of distracting us and can even cause chronic restlessness. When you reduce the noise of the things around you, you can focus on creating your life."

~ Christiane Northrup, M.D.

Chapter Twenty-Five

Clearing Up Resentments

The feeling of resentment can of course be towards people, but it can also be around life events, situations, or circumstances. If you frequently feel deprived in some way, angry, bitter, fearful, disappointed, hurt, or sad, it is highly likely you could benefit from identifying and releasing resentments.

"Open your heart. Let down the walls you think are protecting you, as they are only limiting you and your connections with others. Open your heart to giving and receiving the love you deserve."

~ Joyce Marter, LCPC

Resentment is anger, pain, hurt, or fear continued from the past. When a person associates a current situation to feelings that were not dealt with in a healthy manner, resentments can surface. Sometimes a particular memory is triggered and he or she is aware of what is happening, but other times the direct connection might not be able to be made. It is only known that the thoughts and emotions are elevated and therefore disproportionate to the present situation. The person usually feels overwhelmed when this occurs. Not clearing and resolving the issue usually creates a repeated cycle of repressing and triggering, and it is cumulative. Therefore, resentment tends to be ongoing and strengthens if not processed in a healthy manner.

Because it takes up space within you, resentment can limit perspective and block abundance from being be received in the present moment. This includes love, positive relationships, joy, peace, health, money, and success. Unfortunately, this tends to guide our lives in undesirable directions, especially if we are not aware. Continued resentment generates and supports negative expectations and fears. It becomes part of how we perceive others and ourselves. In addition, it shifts our outlook on life and the world in unhealthy ways.

Over and over again, I have found that clearing and resolving the past significantly improves everything in life (health, wellbeing, life satisfaction, success, abundance, relationships, and more). We may be reluctant to let things go because allowing them to come up and be released can seem scary, unfamiliar, or uncomfortable. Also, people may be anxious about expressing certain feelings because they have associated them with "inappropriate" behaviors.

It is important to note that repeated resentment that is left unprocessed can be like a poison to the physical body. Continuous repression of one's emotions often culminates into symptoms of anxiety and depression. If this is continual, it can have a negative impact physically, frequently within the digestive tract, but many other areas as well.

When illness arises, some people do awaken and slowly begin acknowledging that they cannot simply just escape the past. Again, the effect is cumulative as more time passes. One may come to a point of "hitting bottom" where it becomes glaringly obvious that it must be addressed. I urge you to act before this happens as doing this type of work is usually much more manageable when it is more of a choice than a requirement. It is important to listen to your body, mind, and emotions now, tend to the "messages" that are coming up, and take care of yourself.

As far as new resentments go, one way to prevent them is to address concerns right as they happen. Through our healing, transformation, and growth journeys, we undoubtedly become more aware of our feelings and what we need for ourselves. We learn to set limits and boundaries with others, and make decisions ensuring self-protection. We know when we feel hurt, angry, or afraid, and begin to release and channel feelings in healthier ways when they arise. We put things more into perspective before strong "negative" emotions get too attached and associated with a situation. We acknowledge positive aspects of our lives (what really matters to us) and focus on those. Many additional ideas in this book can also assist along the lines of defending against developing new resentments and resolving past feelings of resentment.

As far as forgiveness goes, it is important to note that choosing to forgive those who you feel have harmed you in the past does not necessarily have to mean you are excusing or forgetting what they did (or did not do). You just may simply want to end the feelings of anger, fear, and hurt that keep surfacing due their past actions (or inaction), and you are now fully aware that the act of forgiveness will contribute significantly to your own personal health, healing, and sense of power over your own life.

"Anger is an acid that can do more harm to the vessel in which it is stored than to anything on which it is poured".

~ Mark Twain

Interestingly, I have found that the most significant and necessary work along the lines of resentment usually relates to self-forgiveness. The idea of forgiving (or accepting) yourself may bring up fears of repeating the past or continuing unwanted behaviors. There may also be thoughts that others will be upset or hurt if you openly face the truth. When, in reality, self-acceptance, self-love, and forgiveness, offer much more healthy self-discipline, feelings of peace and joy, as well as powerful life-altering positive growth opportunities.

Being open to and participating in deep spiritual work can often help clear up resentments and judgments, creating profound shifts in perception, getting one to see things in a completely different light. Therefore also see the "Spiritual Counseling, Guidance, and Education" chapter of this book (among other chapters) to learn more about how to clear up resentments.

Chapter Twenty-Six

Resistance and Self-Sabotage

What are you resisting? This is a normal part of any growth process and is quite common. You may have to do some soul searching to identify what behaviors, thoughts, and feelings may signal your resistance to any healing activities or therapeutic recommendations, and overcome them. It is true that I do not expect you to be able to follow every single suggestion in this book (because there will be some activities that are not possible for you, given your specific conditions or current circumstances, and there are scores of ideas here), however I do expect you to make a good faith effort to research and actually begin (and complete) many activities that resonate with you. If any resistance comes up and it is from an angle of self-sabotage, you will need to do everything you can to work though that issue and remove any blockages to your healing. Some of this is deep in the subconscious mind. It is likely that much of it is outside your current awareness. You may find you need assistance in order to identify and completely clear out those old sabotaging "programs".

Self-sabotage can stem from anger at self. Sometimes it occurs because you are not putting yourself first. The anger then causes negative thoughts, feelings, and behaviors directed inward (like the old saying "beating yourself up"), which is prime breeding ground for illness. This can be quite subtle to detect yet extremely destructive nonetheless. Resistance can even be as simple as being in a healthy body seeming foreign to you and something in which you are not (or no longer) "familiar", therefore it can feel strange or "unsafe" once physical healing begins. You might feel anger at your body for not working "right". Self-sabotage can also come in the form of obsessive thoughts (such as constant thoughts of "Did I leave the stove on?" as you go to do something that is supposed to be fun, relaxing, or restorative). I urge you to open your mind to any indication that this may be occurring, and remedy the situation as soon as possible. Awareness is the first step and it is important. When you increase your insight and self-knowledge you can identify and then release the core beliefs or feelings that are fueling the resistance or self-sabotage. Then you can use specific affirmations to begin combating the unwanted thoughts, feelings, and behaviors, such as: "I feel different now and I am allowing the change in my body and in my life", "I absolutely deserve 100% vibrant health", "I am open to all healing from all positive sources and I feel good", "It is crucial for me to completely relax and enjoy all of my therapy and leisure activities", and "I love and nurture my body".

"Your life is a printout of your subconscious program… We can re-write the subconscious".

~ Bruce Lipton, Ph.D.

Please always remember that you can purge the sabotaging programs and blockages to your healing. They can be replaced with mindsets that encourage what you want in life.

Interestingly, there is a program called "15 Minute Manifestation" which claims to dissolve limiting and sabotaging beliefs that are deep in the subconscious mind. This can be powerful in reversing the cycles of negativity and therefore creating (and attracting) all the abundance you desire in your life. This program takes longer than just 15 minutes (which is good), but you can do it on your own and at the time of this writing it is low cost. Therefore, it might be a good option for those whom are currently short on time and money.

It is important to note that with physical symptoms, some could have played a necessary and protective role for you in the past. Maybe there was some type of ongoing abuse in your home long ago. Therefore, perhaps something such as a feeling of tightness in your abdominal area was once a "protection" of sorts for you. Maybe it signaled to your body and mind that there was danger near, and it acted as a much-needed "shield" at that time, to block out everything that was going on around you. You are grown now. You are strong, with the knowledge and power to protect yourself. The constant shield no longer serves you. It definitely does not serve your highest good now. You can let it go and relax! You are safe now. Go ahead and let in goodness from all positive sources. It will heal you.

"The soul journey inward is when we are invited to cast aside beliefs and behaviors that no longer serve us and release all tendencies toward victimhood, stagnation, passivity, and self-destruction that keep us

disempowered or cause frustration and suffering to ourselves and others.

This is no easy task, and one in which we can use all the divine support

possible to help us on our way. It is a time to pray."

~ Sonia Choquette

Deep in the subconscious mind there can also be programs stemming from wanting revenge or from guilt feelings. For revenge, it could actually be something such as "I'm sick because of you... See what you did to me?" With guilt, it can be like "karma" where you subconsciously are drawing into your life exactly what you think you may be to "blame" for in another person's life.

I could not complete this chapter without touching upon "secondary gains" issues. Is there something you are gaining from having an illness or a significant problem? Perhaps you receive disability payments, or have applied for those benefits? Maybe you attract more attention from your spouse (or specific pals on your social media page) when you are in pain? Whatever it is, identify it, and propose an even better "solution" to your subconscious mind. Keep telling yourself that you can bring in much more money by doing work that resonates with you. You can also attract even more attention (and genuine love) by performing positive acts such as helping others and sending out love. Therefore, some affirmations to continue repeating could include: "I have meaningful and fulfilling work that pays well and aligns with my purpose" or "I receive attention and love in positive healthy ways that support my highest good".

After some time working on these issues, if you still continue to feel like something keeps interfering with your completed healing or problem resolution, I suggest you begin viewing Michael Golzmane videos online (see the "Spiritual Counseling, Guidance, and Education" chapter for more information). If Michael's services have resonated with you but you are feeling the need to take it even further, "Chris Kehler Holistic" is an option. Website: chriskehler.net. He is an Energy/Bio-Spiritual Healer. Again, just to be clear here, he has called himself "The Alternative to the Alternative"!

Chapter Twenty-Seven

Planning For the Worst, and Then Expecting the Best

I f you have a serious health issue, I advise that you to plan for the worst but then completely forget about it and absolutely anticipate the very best! In the past, when I discussed concerns about my health briefly with husband, he put me at ease by saying "We will figure this all out together". I said we need to have a plan for the worst case-scenario (such as: childcare for my son; training our son to do certain tasks on his own; accepting that our RV would then have to be sold; get used to the idea of moving to a smaller house; begin unloading all the unnecessary "stuff" around the house which will make it easier in the future; think about whom could be asked for help; realize that disability benefits might have to be accessed), then absolutely forget about it! It was also evident that I was starting to experience hair loss. At that point I purchased some pretty hats and head coverings. In addition, I researched where one could obtain a high-quality wig, in order to know exactly where to go if necessary. I wanted to do this all before the hair loss became more rapid, because at that point I would have been too devastated to focus on even figuring out what to do. Therefore, I was prepared should it start happening more rapidly. I could then relax because there was nothing more to do! I was relieved, with much less anxiety, after discussing with my husband and planning. The fear definitely dissipated! On a side-note, because of my healing activities, my hair stopped falling out and new growth actually began as well! We have not needed to downsize to a smaller house (in fact we actually upgraded to a home of our dreams), and have kept our RV and continue to take all kinds of trips.

"It's ok to have fears and doubts. It is. They're reminders of our humanness, of our ability to experience a full range of emotions. It's good to acknowledge them, it's just not great to dwell on them. Because when we dwell on the nasty negatives, we're not leaving space for the amazing positives that really want to come and hang out with us."

~ Skylar Liberty Rose

Also, along these lines, always remember, it is a known fact that most of the things we worry about never even happen! I often say this to my clients, and as they recall what they have worried about in the past they confirm this is definitely true in their own lives.

"FEAR pulls us out of the moment. When you are feeling fear, you are usually NOT in the moment, but rather in an imagined future, and when you are not in the moment, you are disconnected from your COURAGE and your True Self. BREATHE. Come back to NOW."

~ Dr. Barbara DeAngelis

After "planning for the worst and hoping for the best", it is helpful to practice what is called "thought-stopping". Re-focusing the mind will be essential for you if you are having any fear about the future. Remember that fear feeds illness, although it is quite understandable as I had quite a bit myself, and I have to admit it did help in motivating me to dive deeply into healing activities. But I knew that experiencing fear on a continual basis would not be good for me. It was clear that after "planning for the worst" I had to stop all fear about the future. I am really thankful I did because again my life is turning out much different than anything I was worried about! To re-focus the mind, it is helpful to incorporate all senses. Use anything that gives you pleasure (beautiful views, great music, amazing aromas, soothing skin sensations), as well as your positive affirmations. Those fearful negative thoughts about the future will quickly melt away!

It is important to note here that over-identifying with a specific disease or problem can have detrimental effects. If you find that the name of your condition often flashes into your mind, then imagine the word(s) on a black board instead. Then immediately visualize someone completely erasing everything and it being 100% gone, ERASED.

"A medical diagnosis is not a 'final' answer. It's an opinion. Yes,

perhaps an informed one, but take it as that, an opinion. With a

diagnosis often comes a 'prognosis' - what to expect from the future.

Again, still an opinion. YOU remain in control of your destiny.

Sometimes in order to heal we have to let go of everything we've been told,

everything we read, everything we believe, sadly because those are often

negative, fearful, thoughts, memories and experiences".

~ Nicolas Ortner

Chapter Twenty-Eight

Balancing the Chakras, and Using Healing Crystals and Stones

E ven though there is not much formal scientific evidence as of yet backing the therapeutic effectiveness of chakra balancing and working with crystals and stones, I still think these types of activities can be an important addition to other therapies and your overall recovery plan if you are open to it.

If you have not worked at all with your chakras, I believe it would be beneficial to get them checked and balanced by a qualified healer. If you are having any health issues, chances are your chakras need attention. It also might require multiple appointments in order to get them working correctly on an ongoing basis. You can also learn how to balance them on your own in order to assist the healing process. "Chakra balancing", like many terms in energy healing, does not really have a standard definition. It indicates a process that increases the healthy flow of energy through the chakras and the entire energy field of the body. It is said that a healthier flow creates increased physical, mental, emotional, and spiritual health. To make it easier for my own chakra balancing, I went ahead and purchased full sets of chakra stones to use while meditating (as well as other uses). I have gotten some of my stones through various shops on Etsy.com. You may also check your local shops for crystals and stones. Sometimes healers actually have them available at their offices. There are also internet sites which explain chakras in detail, their locations within the body, and where to place your crystals while meditating. It is important to obtain stones which help with your particular spiritual, healing, and chakra balancing needs (it will usually be the ones which resonate with you).

Working on suggestions in this book can naturally balance your chakras. Additional quick ways to align them and clear out negative energy include touching a tree (or sitting at the base of a tree leaning up against it) as well as walking or standing barefoot directly on the earth (also called "earthing"). These activities work on your base (root) chakra, which can then help balance the rest of them. A healthy root chakra contributes directly to physical and financial health as well as feelings of safety and security. These activities not only recalibrate your base chakra, but they help clear EMF's from your body (from cell phones, wireless devices, electronics, and computers). When you cannot get outside, imagine touching a tree or walking directly on the earth. This will still give you a feeling that helps balance the body, increase positive energy, and neutralize unhealthy energy.

The vitality of our Etheric Body (our energy body) is extremely important. The Etheric Body is crucial because blockages of energy affect the counterpart (the physical body) and can cause health problems. All the parts are interconnected so that any problem in our energy body eventually seeps into the physical. There also is of course a strong mind-body link, each affecting the other.

Interestingly, cultures throughout the globe have had different names for the vital life force energy that exists within our physical bodies and is abundant within the universe. The Chinese call it qi (or it is sometimes spelled chi, as it is pronounced), while Asian Indians seem to label it as prana. Ancient Eastern cultures explored this phenomenon identifying certain energies and developed systems which began spiritual and physical disciplines that access, balance, and strengthen life force energy. Ayurvedic terms include gunas, doshas, and vayus. Under "yoga" are chakras, mantras, and mudras. To attain the flowing life force of qi, there are the meridians and the essential balance of yin and yang. The Etheric Body is essentially made out of this vital force. Any method you use to access this energy can be highly beneficial to your overall health.

Again, our Etheric Body (vital life force energy) can become blocked. While living the course of our lives (such as through everyday activities and thoughts), our Etheric Body can lose health and vitality. This energy comes to us through our environment, what we breathe, our food, from "Source", and more. It can be of a higher vibration or a lower vibration.

One of the main things that can obstruct flow and block the Etheric Body is our thoughts, because they are actually composed of energy. They exist as a vibration, either high and healthy (positive thoughts), or low and unhealthy (negative thoughts). Anxious thoughts have the lowest vibrations (especially fearful ones), and when we continuously have them, they affect the health of our chakras, our Etheric Body, and lastly even our physical body if they are ongoing. How can you change, control, or quiet down your thoughts? Using positive affirmations repeatedly is one effective way (along with numerous other activities and suggestions contained in this book).

Exercise can also positively affect the energy body. Most of you have felt that vibrant, amazing, healthy feeling after working out. You have just taken in large amounts of oxygen and life force from the environment. All of that circulating around is extremely energetically cleansing.

Our energy and vibration can also become sluggish from a poor diet. We need to consume "living" foods (like fresh whole fruits and vegetables, as well as other raw foods) as this revitalizes the energy body. It is necessary to keep the vital force fresh, flowing, and replenished. Qi is like water, which we also require for vibrant health. We need fresh high-quality water often, and not from a stagnant source. It is the same with qi, as we do not want to consume only highly processed foods due to the stagnant qi.

At our previous home, we were provided with loads of "qi energy" for many months of the year with a wonderful raspberry patch we had in our backyard. They are extremely easy to grow here in Illinois, the act of picking them is energizing, and of course the life force energy that each of them contained when we enjoyed them right after picking was amazing! At our new place I planted more raspberries with the hopes we have the same situation in the future.

As I touched upon, there are positive thought patterns, exercise, and the intake of proper foods and beverages. These are all extremely important, but sometimes they are not quite enough, especially if you already have years of blocked energies within your system. Luckily there are numerous additional ways to clear out or cleanse our energy and chakras, and this book provides plenty of methods. It gives whole lists of things you can do now to vibrate at a higher level of health and help support your chakras.

Putting a Black Tourmaline stone under your pillow can help "cleanse" your Etheric Body while you sleep, as well as the space where you are sleeping. If the stone alone feels too strong, you may add a Rose Quartz to soften the energies. You can keep any stones of choice in an organza bag under your pillow where they will stay nicely.

Black Tourmaline: Simply speaking, Black Tourmaline healing stones are known to protect against and help clear out negative energy of all kinds. They are inexpensive, and you can place them around your house as well as keep them with you in a pocket or bag. You can also hold one while you meditate. Black Tourmaline has been used to cleanse, purify, and transform dense energy into a lighter vibration (transmuting negative energy into usable energy). Like most black stones, it is said to be strong in aiding with grounding, clearing the aura, and balancing chakras as well as meridians. It can help align the energy centers of the body and channel healing light throughout the system. It is used to increase physical vitality, dispersing tension and stress. It is said to promote self-confidence and alleviate feelings of unworthiness and victimization. It is known for attracting inspiration, compassion, tolerance of others, and prosperity, as well as increasing clear, rational thought processes. It has been used as a "mental healer", helping to balance the right and left hemispheres of the brain and transmuting negative thought patterns into positive ones. Black Tourmaline is considered a shamanic stone, said to provide protection during ritual work. It was also traditionally used to indicate a positive direction in which to proceed.

It is a known fact that Black Tourmaline is electrical in nature (magnetic electricity). It is used as a "shield" around the body to deflect and dispel negative energies, entities, or destructive forces. It is suggested to use this stone when you feel surrounded by negativity, particularly beneficial if you are in a large crowd, if you are around someone who is constantly complaining, or if you are in a place that might not be healthy for you.

These stones can help "clear" dwellings of past negative situations (such as an experience with illness). If your house has a "heavy" feeling or if you occasionally do not want to go home, these stones can definitely help begin to turn that around!

Black Tourmaline also is known for protecting against cell phone emanations, electromagnetic disturbance, radiation, and environmental pollutants (people with autoimmune conditions are often sensitive to those types of energies). I place it in front of my computer and it assists in keeping beneficial energy resonating throughout my personal energy field.

This black stone has also been known to aid in detoxification, diabetes, lung conditions, and energy flow. It can be helpful for dyslexia, spinal adjustments, hand-eye coordination, and balancing of male and female energies. Black Tourmaline has also been known to assist in defending against debilitating diseases, treating arthritis, and relieving pain. It has been used to help strengthen the immune system, as well as heart and adrenal glands. It is said to treat motion sickness, and increase the sense of smell. If you need full concentration for a task, it can help you wake up as well. In addition, Black Tourmaline is said to soothe anxiety, fear, paranoia, over-attachment, and obsession, as well as alleviate issues such as panic attacks and claustrophobia. It has also been used to assist with fear of doctors and dentists. It can be a valuable stone for crises and periods of extreme stress.

When I feel tightness in my neck, shoulders, or back and I am not able to get a message, I place a large Black Tourmaline stone on the area where it feels tight. After relaxing for a while with the stone placed on that area, including positive healing intent, the tightness dissipates!

Black Obsidian: These stones are said to have many of the same healing qualities as Black Tourmaline. They are used to help clear any psychic "smog" created within the aura, and for protection. They are said to have powerful metaphysical properties that shield against negativity. It can be an excellent stone to use when you have been doing spiritual or healing work, as it can help ground you. The resonance within the base chakra is quite strong. It has a vibration that can aid spiritual grounding, by helping you to move unneeded energy down via the earth chakra.

This black stone may assist you in releasing disharmony that has built up in daily life (and during work on yourself), including resentment, anger, and fear. This stone is also said to help remove any negativity caused by other people's strong emotions. These stones may assist you to seal your aura against future problems, and may aid in releasing yourself from any negative attachments that you may have unintentionally acquired. Therefore they can be helpful stones to keep within your auric field.

If you are open to it, the vibration of this stone has been known to aid spiritual communication, and may help you find a spirit guide. For centuries they have been used to connect with spiritual realms. These stones are highly protective and can be helpful if you are doing any work of that sort. This stone has a strong vibration said to aid in receiving answers to questions. By asking a question and listening, you may receive an answer. You can ask about relationships, finances, career, or health issues. When looking into a shiny piece of the stone in the right light (usually low light is best) you may see images of loved ones in spirit or pick up the vibration of their thoughts via your feelings, similar to clairsentience. It is said to stimulate prophecy and may assist with seeing future scenes reflected in the stone.

If you believe in past lives, Black Obsidian stones are used to aid in past life healing and may help with issues relating to past misuse of power. If you have come to this life in order to resolve a past life issue, by placing the stone on the third eye chakra and asking about this, you may discover a purpose for being here. These stones have the potential to help you release whatever may be blocking you from getting what you want out of this life.

This stone's energy tends to bring to the forefront negative attributes or situations you may have been wanting to ignore. They are known to have a particularly strong and confronting vibration of truth and can work quite quickly. Once you perceive these issues, the energy of this stone can "push" you to make changes. This can sometimes feel frustrating, especially if the change cannot be fully completed at that moment. But I have found that if you keep showing even a small amount of progress toward what the stone is pushing you towards, the frustration will subside.

If you are a healer assisting clients in clearing unhealthy energy, it is possible to take the negativity into your auric field. Using this stone may aid both you and your clients as it is said to be a cleanser of psychic "smog" created within the aura.

These stones have a strong psychological healing energy for many people. They are known to aid the release of addictions, eating disorders, negative behaviors, and emotional blockages. Black Obsidian may help you discover the spiritual aspects of unconditional love and use this positive energy to improve your life. Used with intent, it is said to aid physical ailments such as hardening of the arteries, joint pain, arthritis, cramps, and circulation problems.

Shungite: These stones have been known for containing healing powers incomparable to any others. They are said to help with detoxifying and purifying the body by absorbing and eliminating negative energies or anything that is health hazardous to humans. Shungite fills the aura with light, allowing only positive and healing energies to come into contact with the body. It can help bring to the forefront positive blessings and outcomes, leading you into knowing what is beneficial for a healthier and improved future for yourself. Please note that this can also push you towards awareness of anything negative that you were resistant to seeing in your life, and therefore it has the potential to create large life transformations. These changes, although needed, can sometimes cause what initially seems like an "upheaval", such as it being suddenly crystal clear that divorce is necessary, and following through on that. Certain types of actions, when necessary, can later promote healing on all levels.

Shungite is said to cleanse and align all particles within the body, helping to purify, normalize, induce recovery, and promote growth in living things. A large sphere can help in the process of extracting and releasing subconscious feelings, thought processes, and memories. This helps clear dysfunctional patterns, which manifest as negativity, emotional difficulties, or even disease. Consider placing some Shungite stones on an affected area of your body, along with healing intent, and you will likely see an accelerated resolution to the problem. It is carbon-based and absorbent. It has been used for viruses and infections within the body. If you are looking for more of a full body healing, try simply holding or meditating with the stones, along with positive intent. The Shungite properties are also said to be beneficial for reducing stress and anxiety, soothing insomnia, and boosting energy. Healers use Shungite to assist in alleviating a wide variety of physical complaints such as heart difficulties, allergies, skin diseases, arthritis, as well as for hair and skin rejuvenation.

Especially beneficial in protection from EMFs, Shungite has been known to be useful in absorbing radiation. Many people place Shungite next to or near their electronics (such as computers, microwaves, refrigerators, cell phones, and televisions) to help provide a shield from EMFs. A sizable Shungite sphere can "protect" a large area of your home. Shungite is used for psychic protection as well.

Hematite: Natural hematite healing stones are used for grounding, and there is uniqueness in the protective energy of Hematite due to its mirror-like shine, which is said to repel negativity. The positive energy has been used to balance auras and align chakras, as it can help to bring together and balance the mind, body, and spirit (magnetic qualities). Hematite can assist one to embody high vibration energy while at the same time releasing any unnecessary energy. Specific physical problems that seem to be aided by using Hematite include the action to strengthen the liver and support the health of the spleen. It is said to be helpful with problems in the blood system and blood disorders (such as anemia), and is known for assisting the body in absorbing iron. Hematite is said to aid in the formation of new red blood cells, helping the production of blood within the bone marrow. It has also been used to help to ensure that broken bones or fractures heal properly. It may assist with leg cramps as well.

In addition to the physical healing properties of Hematite, it has been known to soothe emotions which can keep the user more focused and "in control". It has also been used in overcoming addictions, anxiety, and insomnia. Hematite is known as the "stress stone," according to crystal energy therapist, Karen Ryan. Ryan says to carry your Hematite stone in your pocket or leave it under your pillow at night. It can help your thoughts to be more focused, balanced, and clear, resulting in increased communication and self-esteem. Hematite crystals have been considered useful "female" stones, assisting shy women to have increased confidence. If you use it at the solar plexus (also known as the power chakra), the energy may enhance your willpower and personal magnetism. Hematite has also been used to remedy yin imbalances, and can also assist in releasing negativity and feeling more at peace. It is said to prevent absorbing the negativity of others. You can also use the stone as a decorative object or in jewelry.

Amethyst: This is a favorite of mine. It is considered to be a stone of spirituality, contentment, peace, and healing. It can help raise a lower vibration. When needed, you can try lifting your mood by putting on some beautiful Amethyst jewelry, drinking Amethyst "gem water" (more details are given under the Rose Quartz section of this chapter), or meditating holding a piece of the crystal. Amethyst has been used to attract love and happiness. It offers powerful protection on the spiritual planes of existence, so if you are doing any of that type of work, incorporate Amethyst. Being a powerfully psychic stone, it is associated with the crown chakra which helps in the connection to spiritual realms. It has been used as a bridge for those seeking spiritual guidance, healing, or protection. Amethyst is believed to help people overcome alcoholism and other addictions. It also may assist one in recovering from the effects of a hangover.

If you want to have a night filled with dreams, place an Amethyst stone under your pillow. This works and I have proof. One night, one of my larger Amethyst stones got out from under my pillow and somehow got over to my husband's side of the bed. That morning he said "Did you say you had stones under your pillow in order to have more dreams, because one ended up under my back during the night and I had tons of dreams!" Ok, this came from a mechanical engineer who did not tend to believe in such things! Well he does now. Using Amethyst can help produce multiple good vivid dreams throughout the night. Having a calming yet spiritually protective energy makes it beneficial for any type of dream work. It can also assist in overcoming insomnia and/or nightmares. It makes a wonderful addition to herbal dream pillows.

Rose Quartz: This is another one of my favorite stones. Like I said previously, it has a vibration of love. Love of all types. It is connected with the heart chakra. Due to being one of the more "absorbent" types of crystals, you can keep Rose Quartz in your hand while meditating and imagine all negative energy flowing into the stone. Think of everything that may be interfering with your healing and imagine all of that being absorbed by the stone. Rose Quartz also can enhance the use of your positive affirmations. This stone is said to aid in opening the heart and healing old wounds, leaving one feeling more balanced emotionally. Rose Quartz is used to comfort and help one through crisis. It is great for soothing grief and loss, during "heartache". Gem water (gem elixir) can be made from Rose Quartz to give a nice feeling of well-being. I use the "indirect method" when making my gem water (stones do not go directly into the drinking water). Work with a qualified healer before beginning a regimen of gem water, or at least do some in-depth research first, from trusted sources. As a side note, I love using VOSS® (in glass water bottles), which is found in supermarkets, for creating my gem water. Another way to use this stone is as a pendant on a medium-length necklace as it will stay directly over the heart area.

"When we have a well-balanced heart chakra, we care about others and feel cared about in return. We feel intimately connected to society as a whole and freely express kindness, affection, and generosity. We are able to love unconditionally, recognizing the goodness in people regardless of their behavior. We are able to give love without expectation or ulterior motives, and in this way can ease suffering of even the most traumatized individuals. You can recognize someone with a well-balanced heart by his or her authenticity and openness."

~ Heather McCutcheon

Aquamarine: Interestingly, Aquamarine stones are said to help calm overreactions of the immune system and autoimmune diseases. They have been known to aid in decreasing old, self-defeating patterns that no longer serve, clearing blocked communication (including spiritual), and promoting self-expression (supports the throat chakra). Aquamarine can help one to understand and interpret underlying emotions. It has a soothing energy which makes it perfect for courage and protection. Aquamarine can also work with the heart chakra, encouraging tolerance of others, and helping one realize his or her innermost truth. It is great to use while meditating as it can bring knowledge from the higher self to be used in daily life, open the intuitive mind, and carry in higher frequency information through the third eye chakra. The energies of Aquamarine can help with chakra balancing as well as contribute to one recognizing and connecting with the natural flow of life. During spiritual work, Aquamarine has been said to repel dark energy. Aquamarine is used for sore throats, swollen glands, and thyroid problems. It can help harmonize pituitary, thyroid, regulating hormones, and growth. This stone has a "tonic" effect and is said to strengthen the body's cleansing organs and aid the eyes, jaw, teeth, and stomach.

Tiger's Eye: This can be a powerful stone to include for manifesting an increase in money. It has been known to stimulate taking action, enhancing creativity, and attracting abundance. It is an excellent stone for prosperity of all kinds. Work with it for a while with positive intent, give it some time, and see what happens!

This stone has been known to bring about good decision-making, unclouded by emotions. It can help with more easily seeing both sides of a situation, beneficial if you are any type of mediator.

Tiger's Eye is a contradiction in some ways. While it is "energizing", it can also be calming. It has helped me fall asleep quickly in the past! This stone can aid harmony and balance, assist in the release of fear and anxiety, and has been known to give courage, self-confidence, and strength of will. It may benefit individuals suffering from mental health conditions. Traditionally it was carried to guard against curses or ill-wishing,

Like many of the healing stones, it can be used in jewelry-making (makes a nice looking bracelet). You can also meditate with it or just keep in your purse, pocket, or in front of your computer while working.

- For information on the Carnelian stone see the "Dan tien" chapter.

Books for further learning on stones and crystals (recommended by shaman, Monica Tyler):
- "The Book of Stones" by Robert Simmons and Naisha Ahsian.
- "Cunningham's Encyclopedia of Crystal, Gem, and Metal Magic" by Scott Cunningham.
- "The Encyclopedia of Crystals", "The Crystal Bible", and "Crystal Prescriptions" all by Judy Hall.

A few places to purchase healing stones and crystals (including chakra sets):
- Various shops on Etsy.com (such as moonlightmystiques)
- 13Moons.com
- There are many local shops around the country with great selections of stones, crystals, and other items which promote healing. One nice thing about brick and mortar shops is that there are likely people there who can answer all types of questions for you. For example, there is a wonderful shop in downtown Geneva, Illinois, called LDH Harmony Style (ldhharmony.com)

Make sure the healing crystals and stones you purchase are high-quality and are not heat treated or colored in any way. The best crystals and stones have nice color and are all natural.

It is important to note that certain stones are used for Feng Shui purposes and are said to change the energy in a home and help alter life's issues, such as with financial woes or health concerns.

Most healers believe it is a good idea to "cleanse" your stones and crystals periodically, in order for them to "work" at peak level. I cleanse all of my newly purchased stones in order to clear out any old energy. To do this, I rinse briefly with cold water (with the intent of "previous energies" to run down the drain), and then place in a sun-lit area (like a windowsill) for a small amount of time (however, do not let the stones get too much direct sunlight as you do not want to them to lose color). Other ideas for cleansing are leaving them in the light of a full moon, or burying in the ground for a brief time. Some also say salt water works well (just do not soak crystals for too long as it can ruin them). For activating a newly obtained stone and aligning it with your own energy and intentions, you can hold it in your left hand (your "receiving" hand) and make statements such as "I activate this crystal/stone to support my highest good and dedicate it to my highest good". Also include any associated goals you may have.

Keep in mind that too many crystals and stones stored in the bedroom is not the best idea as it is likely you mostly want to relax and sleep in there. Too many amplified energies may not help with that goal! That said, stones like Amethyst, Rose Quartz, and Tiger's Eye are usually gentle enough to continually have at your bedside, or with you while resting.

Healing crystals and stones are believed to carry healing powers and life force energy from the earth and sky. Interestingly, their therapeutic properties were documented more than 3,500 years ago by Ancient Egyptians, as well as

Asian cultures. That said, crystals and stones are not intended to diagnose, cure, or prevent any disease or condition. The suggested uses in this publication are to be researched in order to determine if any are applicable for your personal use, as an "add-on" to augment your current treatments and healing activities. I am not trying to suggest they alone are an effective treatment or cure for any disease or condition. You will need to of course consult your health care provider for diagnosis or treatment.

Chapter Twenty-Nine

Reiki Treatments

Reiki (pronounced "ray-key") can be a highly beneficial integrative therapy. People generally start feeling better quite quickly with Reiki, as anxiety, "lower" emotions, and pain often decrease or are released.

People then tend to feel hopeful about regaining their health, and are more able and willing to incorporate additional needed interventions and lifestyle changes. Reiki therapy also often clears the mind of any unnecessary "clutter", which can assist when evaluating the sometimes conflicting recommendations one tends to receive as a patient. Reiki can help with making important treatment decisions with more confidence, and assist people in becoming more involved in their own health, which is always beneficial.

Fortunately, now, many people are beginning to practice techniques that improve mental and physical conditions. More are incorporating lifestyle changes such as meditation, exercise, and enhanced nutrition. As this is done, awareness often starts to develop concerning the flow of subtle energies in and around the body, and the connection with these energies and one's health and wellbeing. This follows the ancient idea of "life force energy" as the cause of health, and its lack as the cause of illness. The existence of life force energy, and the necessity for it to flow freely in and around the body to maintain vitality, has actually been studied and acknowledged by scientists as well as health care providers, and is of increasing interest.

Again, our bodies are composed not only of physical elements, but also subtle energy systems through which life force energy flows. Reiki follows the idea that energy "bodies" surround the physical body and assist in processing thoughts and emotions. These energy bodies have centers (chakras), which work like valves that allow life force to circulate through the physical, mental, emotional, and spiritual bodies. We also have meridians which are like streams carrying our life force energy throughout our physical bodies, to nourish and assist in balancing systems and functions.

When our life force decreases or is blocked, we are more likely to have health problems. However, if it is high and free flowing, we more easily heal, increase feelings of wellbeing, and maintain health. Emotional stress blocks the flow of life force energy. This is often caused by "lower" thoughts and feelings that get trapped in one's subtle energy system. These include anger, fear, sadness, hurt, and distrust. Medical research has actually determined that continual negative stress can disrupt the body's natural ability to repair and protect itself. Amazingly, the American Institute of Stress estimates that 75%-95% of all doctor visits are the result of reaction to stress. The physical effects of unreleased stress range from minor aches and pains, to major health concerns (such as digestive disorders, heart disease, skin conditions, and respiratory issues).

Reiki is a healing technique based on the idea that through touch, the therapist can channel energy into the client. This then activates the natural healing processes of the body and helps restore physical health and emotional wellbeing. By creating deep relaxation, Reiki assists the body in releasing stress, tension, and repressed emotions. Because of this, it promotes healing and health. It also helps with pain reduction. The word Reiki contains two Japanese words. "Rei" means "the Wisdom of God or the Higher Power" and "Ki" means "life force energy". Therefore, Reiki means "spiritually guided life force energy". This system of healing is a technique for transmitting this subtle energy to yourself and others through the hands into the human energy system. Reiki restores balance and vitality by relieving the physical and emotional effects of unreleased stress. It opens blocked meridians and chakras, as well as clears the energy bodies. Reiki can accelerate healing, actually assist the body in clearing toxins, balance the flow of subtle energy by releasing blockages, connect one to knowing what is truly important in life, and increase communication with the "inner healer" that is in all of us.

Reiki aims to leave clients relaxed and at peace, and it can feel like a comforting warm sensation and gentle light flowing through and surrounding the body. It is powerful, yet gentle and nurturing. Reiki treats the body, emotions, mind, and spirit all as a whole. It can be an effective addition to any other healing method a client may be utilizing. It is a simple, natural, and safe method of spiritual healing and self-improvement that can benefit anyone that is open to the process. You can learn to tap into the unlimited supply of life force energy to improve health and enhance the quality of life by actions such as learning Reiki, or by having sessions with a practitioner. In addition, healing stones and crystals are often incorporated and used in this form of treatment.

I recently received sessions from a local Reiki Master. She also does chakra balancing and has intuitive abilities (including services such as Akashic records). I was in awe about how much actual heat was present during the initial session! She said it all came from her hands and there was no other heat source such as an electric heating pad. It was definitely some kind of powerful influence that came through, what I felt coming from her hands. During the first session, it seemed as if I was actually in a peaceful field, with the light of the sun on my face, and a deep "knowing" that everything was going to be just fine. The session left me feeling extremely relaxed, with clarity about what is most important in life, realizing I no longer needed to feel any anxiety or fear about anything, and instilling a feeling of happiness (and how much I deserved all of that). We also addressed the chakras during the process. I felt peaceful, grounded, balanced, cared for, and loved by the Universe. During additional sessions, she did a grief extraction of sorts where certain emotions came to the surface in a much-needed way. A blockage was also removed for more "receiving" (apparently the left hand/shoulder receives, and the right gives). She also helps people who are having various issues with their homes where she pinpoints the actual problems and then steps toward resolving them can begin.

The following is a quote from my colleague Sabrina Gosmire, LCPC, who is a Psychotherapist and Reiki provider at Oak Brook Counseling & Wellness, LTD, in Illinois:

"I see Reiki as a wonderful tool for relaxation, meditation and understanding the body's wisdom. I have integrated Reiki mainly as a stress management/meditation practice. Simply stated, Reiki is a form of prayer. Intentions, guided meditation and a safe place is created for a person to listen to their body and for the body to do healing. Some of the resources that have been helpful for me are the following: Reiki for Dummies, Psychotherapeutic Reiki, and the work of Deepak Chopra, Louise Hay, and Miguel Ruiz. I also have studied Dr. Jon Kabit-Zinn, Dr. Ron Seigel and Thich Nhat Hanh's work ... One of my favorite websites is www.mindfulness-solution.com."

Chapter Thirty

Pranic Healing

L ike Reiki, Pranic healing is an energy-based modality. Though both use somewhat different techniques, they use the same source of energy to restore health and wellbeing. The main intervention used in pranic healing is cleansing and energizing whereas in Reiki the practitioner channels divine energy.

Pranic healing utilizes prana (life force) to repair, restore, balance, harmonize, and alter the body's energy processes. It addresses both emotional as well as physical imbalances. This invisible yet powerful vital energy keeps the body alive and maintaining vibrant health. In acupuncture, Traditional Chinese Medicine (TCM) refers to this type of energy as qi. Pranic healing is based on the principle that the body is self-repairing and the process is accelerated by increasing this life force that is readily available from the air, sun, and earth. Life energy or prana is always surrounding us, therefore, a practitioner can draw it in easily from his or her surroundings. Pranic healing is actually quite simple, and does not usually involve any instruments, substances, or medicines.

Physical contact is not even typically required because the practitioner is working on the "energy body" only. This energy body (some also refer to it as aura), is said to be the blueprint that surrounds and penetrates the physical body. It actually brings in life energy and distributes it throughout the physical body. Pranic healing works on the energy body because it follows the premise that physical ailments first appear as energetic disruptions in the aura before manifesting as actual physical symptoms or conditions. This pervasive energy that surrounds, penetrates, sustains, and helps to heal the physical body, also can affect emotions, relationships, ability to handle stress, and even financial matters.

Chapter Thirty-One

Dan tien

Dan tien is a term also referred to as "energy center", "sea of qi", or "elixir field" within the body. Traditionally speaking, a dan tien is considered to be a center of qi or life force energy. Dan tiens are key focal points for meditative and exercise techniques such as qigong, martial arts (such as tai chi), and Traditional Chinese Medicine (TCM) (including acupuncture). The dan tiens are also important in Reiki, Neidan, neigong, tao yin, Taoist sexual practices, and other self-cultivation practices of exercise, breathing, meditation, and spirituality. It is pronounced "don tien". Additional spellings include: "tan tien", "dantian", and "dan t'ian".

The first full description of the lower dan tien referred to the "cinnabar" field (just below the navel) where essence and spirit are said to be stored. It is related to regeneration and sexual energy, menstruation, and semen. The lower dan tien is particularly important as the focal point of breathing techniques, mediation, as well as the center of balance and gravity. Dan tiens can be compared to the Western concepts of "mind" or "spirit". Taoist and

Buddhist teachers often instruct their students to center their minds in the lower dan tien. This is believed to aid control of thoughts and emotions, and "acting from the dan tien" is connected to higher states of awareness or what is called "samadhi".

The principle is that every creature in the universe moves around an internal and external core. The Taoist concept of dan tiens as energy centers is similar to the Asian Indian yoga chakras as key points where prana is stored. Yogic chakras are not so much storage centers, but energetic whirling masses which act as intake and output ports. Many traditions consider the dan tiens and the chakras to be separate, yet cooperative, energetic mechanisms.

Three main dan tiens are typically highlighted:

- Lower dan tien: below the navel (about three finger widths below and two finger widths behind the navel), which is also called "the golden stove" or "cinnabar field", where the process of refining and purifying essence (jing) into vitality (qi) begins.
- Middle dan tien: at the level of the heart, which is also called "the crimson palace", associated with respiration, and health of the internal organs (in particular the thymus gland). This is where qi is refined into spirit and stored.
- Upper dan tien: at the forehead between the eyebrows, or what is considered the third eye, which is also called "the muddy pellet" (associated with the pineal gland). This is where spirit is refined.

The term dan tien, when used by itself, usually refers to the lower dan tien. The lower dan tien has been described to be "like the root of the tree of life". It is often used interchangeably with the Japanese word "hara" (in Chinese it is called "fù") which simply means "belly". In Chinese, Korean, and

Japanese traditions, it is considered the physical center of gravity of the human body and is the essential foundation of one's internal energy (qi). In yoga philosophy, the dan tien is the seat of prana that radiates outwards to the entire body.

How can we strengthen the dan tien? Exercising the movement of dan tien energy can help improve vitality and the health the blood, as well as decrease stagnations in the internal organs. There are effective methods to balance yin and yang in our bodies, help prevent and heal disease, increase longevity, improve the quality of life, nourish energy and the blood, maintain optimism, and strengthen against other people's negative energy. They can also assist in preventing depression and dementia, as well as unwanted stagnations.

Some methods to strengthen and open up the dan tien:

- Standing straightening the spine and organs.
- Sitting up straight.
- Walking with heels down and toes up.

The benefits are said to include:

- Opening up internal organs creating energy and blood flow, and decreasing stagnations.
- Pushing the spine up nourishing the brain preventing dementia, depression, and stagnations.
- Opening up the skeleton and ligaments.
- Creating optimism and reducing stress and anxiety.
- Helping fertility and gynecological problems.
- Assisting the immune system in preventing cancer.
- Improving posture which contributes to overall health.

Qigong and Tai Chi are activities specially designed to make full use of dan tien energy. Certain breathing exercises (see other chapter "The Benefits of Deep Breathing") also help strengthen the all-important dan tien (in addition to many other recommendations in this book such as eating well). Acupuncture from an experienced Licensed Acupuncturist that practices TCM is another option to assist in strengthening dan tien energy. I also use a "proprietary" essential oil mix from my former acupuncturist that I apply daily to the area just below the navel, with the goal of strengthening the lower dan tien. He said that when this energy is further strengthened then the rest of the body will continue to follow, creating overall health. As a side note, I love the scent of the oil, therefore it can be used it as a natural fragrance.

For extra help in "strengthening" the lower dan tien area of the body you may try using Carnelian healing stones. This is a beautiful orange color stone with a fiery "energy". It coordinates with the sacral or spleen chakra and is known to be both an energizing as well as a stabilizing stone. Used with intention, it is said to help build courage, self-esteem, passion, and creativity, which can be useful for those who have to take a "leap of faith" about something. It is known to help strengthen a weak voice therefore it may assist in public speaking. It has been used to provide a connection to the past and assist in healing trauma and emotional wounds that have accumulated in the Etheric Body or the aura and are now manifesting as physical symptoms. It can help bring awareness of feelings, at the same time protecting against fear and releasing sorrow. This stone can assist you in feeling grounded and comfortable with your surroundings. It also said to aid in concentration, memory, analytical capabilities, and precision. Used to increase appetite and celebration, it supports experiencing pleasure, passion, and sexuality. It is regarded as an excellent "career" stone in that it can be helpful in making choices and decisions, as well as increasing ambition and drive. It is said to reveal hidden talents by stimulating curiosity (with inspiration from spiritual realms). Carnelian is believed to warm, cleanse, and purify the blood, and aid the health of the liver and kidneys. It has also been used to assist with menstrual cramps, arthritis, gall bladder issues, and the pancreas. Carnelian is said to strongly influence the reproductive organs hence its connection to the second chakra, and can be useful for lower back issues.

Chapter Thirty-Two

Dream Work

Your nighttime dreams can give insight into concerns you may want to tackle as well as what might need to be released. It can be something to forgive within yourself, a past mistake to make amends for, signify a hurt that needs expressing, a problem that needs addressing, and so on. Dreams can also help you organize the subconscious mind, and in positive and beneficial ways. On a more physical note, I do need to add that sometimes dreams occur due to indigestion (especially recurrent negative ones), so it might be useful to link them to a food (or substance) that you may have ingested that is not working well for you at this time.

I suggest writing down your dreams upon awakening. What I usually do is go by how the dream made me feel, in order to gain more insight, and then go from there. I also try and connect my dreams to anything that is currently going on in my life. Linking symbols and themes to the past can help as well. You can research certain symbols that have been apparent in dreams in order to see what they might have been trying to communicate. Many healers and therapists can also assist with this type of work.

Before going to sleep you can ask the Universe for dreams, and be open to receiving them. Ask for wisdom, insight, and healing (specifically) from your dreams. You can ask to dream about being completely healed so that the subconscious mind gets the clear message (and your body follows), giving your true self more of a chance to emerge. You can ask "healing angels" to guide and protect you while sleeping so that you enjoy only sweet and restorative dreams. Some affirmations to repeat before falling asleep might be: "My dreams heal me", "I am completely 100% vibrantly healthy in all of my dreams", and "My dreams communicate to me how I can heal completely". If you are open to it, you can ask the heavens, God, or your higher self to help if you wish. Also, just before falling asleep, use statements such as "I am dreaming", and it will then often provide.

Using specific healing stones and crystals can also bring about certain types of dreams. For example, as I was working on my throat chakra using the corresponding stones, I was having dreams of confronting others, strong self-expression, and releasing certain thoughts and feelings. This was quite interesting because the healthfulness of the throat chakra is in relation to how honestly one expresses himself or herself. Even suppressing anger (not speaking out when needed) may manifest into a symptom such as laryngitis. Many of us have experienced that "lump in our throats" when do not know how to speak the "right" words in a situation, perhaps even repressing emotions. The throat chakra receives and assimilates information, and encourages truthful authentic expressions, strengthening the healthfulness of the mind, body, and spirit.

If you happen to be suffering from nightmares, as you continue working on your growth, try placing an Amethyst stone under your pillow as it should give you some relief. After doing some research to see which type of stone you may want to use for your dreams for a particular period of time (or specific issue), put the stone in an organza bag and place it under your pillow. Sweet dreams!

- Also see the "Spiritual Counseling, Guidance, and Education" chapter for more on dreams.

Chapter Thirty-Three

Simple Self-Hypnosis for Your Subconscious Mind

Here is an easy self-hypnosis technique to help re-program your subconscious mind and therefore receive more of what you want out of life! Also, by consciously letting go of tension and creating an environment which is peaceful and quiet, our bodies go from an activated mode to a deactivated one, which greatly benefits health and wellbeing.

(A word of caution: self-hypnosis is not recommended for anyone who has a serious mental illness or a history of psychosis.)

1. Schedule a half hour if possible. Find whatever time of day feels right for you, designate it as "self-hypnosis" time, and make sure you will not be disturbed.

2. Wear loose clothes and find a comfortable chair (I use my recliner, but you may choose to sit up straight if that is the only situation you have available or if you are afraid you will fall asleep in a different position). Leave your legs and arms uncrossed as you want your energy to flow freely. Playing meditation music may help you go into hypnosis more easily.

3. Relax, and free your mind and body of any tension or stress. Take three deep breaths and hold each one in for a few seconds before exhaling. Choose a point on the wall and focus on it. It can be a picture, or whatever you desire. Focus on that point, concentrating on your eyelids. Repeat to yourself that they are getting heavier and heavier, and then let them close when you cannot keep them open anymore.

4. Close your eyes and imagine that with each breath you take, your body is filling with relaxation and peace, and with each exhale you are breathing out all stress, worry, tension, irritation, and frustration.

5. Relax your body from head to toe. As you relax all the muscles in your head, scalp, face, and neck, continue with the muscles in your body from top down (paying particular attention to any areas that feel tense), so that you begin to feel like a ragdoll, heavy in the chair.

6. Deepen your relaxation. Visualize or picture a beautiful staircase leading down to a peaceful place. Imagine the stairs and this special place any way you prefer, as long as it helps you to feel relaxed and content. This is where you begin to go fully into hypnosis, and it starts with this staircase. Imagine you are walking down one step at a time, and with each step you take, you are becoming deeper and deeper relaxed. As you count from 10 down to 1, your relaxation intensifies at each step.

7. When you reach the last step, walk into the beautiful peaceful place in your imagination. This is hypnosis. It may feel like you are a bit lightheaded which is normal. This place can be like a dream and can change and shift as much as you like.

8. In this place there is a wall with locked cabinets and each one contains something you want in life. Imagine you are wandering that special place and you find a beautiful key, it may look like a skeleton key or like no other you have seen before (my skeleton key has crystal sparkles). Go over to the wall of locked cabinets. Notice there is one that is glowing brightly as it contains exactly what you want most in life. Use your beautiful key to open it.

9. As you open the special cabinet, imagine it is filled with a powerful light that surrounds and becomes part of you. As you imagine the glowing light shining out from the cabinet and surrounding you, use a positive affirmation to suggest the change or improvement that you want most in your life. Choose from the affirmations in this book (such as "I am 100% vibrantly healthy"), or create your own. Use only positive words and in the present tense. Repeat the statement over and over in your mind. Allow this powerful glowing light to enter your body as you completely absorb it. Spend some time imagining yourself in the new circumstances and picture how you would act now that your behaviors, habits, and life have now all changed. Let this resonate deep within your mind, and really feel it within your core, using all senses.

10. When you are ready, awakening and coming out of hypnosis is simple. Imagine you are returning to the beautiful staircase and walking back up, slowly, one step at a time. Count up from one to ten. With each step you come further out of hypnosis. You become more alert, aware, awake, and full of vibrant health and vitality. Once you reach the tenth

step at the top, slowly open your eyes and tell yourself, "Wide awake, wide awake". This will bring your mind back to the conscious state (it is important to always do this awakening step at the end even if you fall asleep during the hypnosis portion or if you get sidetracked into something else). Then go on with your day, continuing to be full of vibrant health and vitality!

"Embrace everything that you want so you can get more of it."

~ Lisa Nichols, Author

Chapter Thirty-Four

Guided Imagery

Guided Imagery is a fascinating and powerful mind-body technique that is considered a form of hypnosis. Guided imagery and visualization offer tools to direct one's concentration on images held in the mind. These techniques take advantage of the connection between the visual brain and the involuntary nervous system. When the back portion of the brain (the visual cortex) is activated, it can influence physical and emotional states. This, in turn, can help elicit physiologic changes in the body, including bringing one to desired therapeutic goals. Because guided imagery is a mind-body therapy, any stress-related health concern (including high blood pressure, insomnia, anxiety/depression, skin rashes, IBS, or pain related to muscle tension) can be alleviated with this approach. It has also been shown to be beneficial in treating autoimmune disorders, such as RA and Crohn's disease, as well as chronic allergies, hives, and asthma. As you work on healing you will see that as you calm your body down, it is less likely to over-react to whatever is in (or happening in) your environment. The conditions, symptoms, and problems that can benefit from guided imagery therapy seem to be countless.

The therapeutic uses of guided imagery usually fall into three categories:

- Relaxation and stress reduction.

- Active visualization or directed imagery. This is for improving performance, modifying behavior, or influencing outcomes. It can include envisioning an illness being cured.

- Receptive imagery. This is where words and images are brought to consciousness to explore and give information about symptoms, moods, illnesses, or treatments.

Guided imagery can be learned from books, CDs, DVDs, apps, or one can utilize a practitioner to facilitate the techniques. Initially, it involves achieving a state of relaxation. To attain this, most clients begin by lying down or sitting in a comfortable chair, loosening any tight fitting clothes, and turning off all devices. Practitioners often have a room which supports this process. After a client gets comfortable, breathing techniques, music, progressive muscle relaxation, and/or a guided induction is often used to help promote a state of deep tranquility.

A set of instructions or suggestions might then be given to allow one's own images or imagination to navigate toward the method of relieving concerns. This can also include discovering images that have a message about particular symptoms or a condition, which can offer insight, understanding, or better management of physical issues. Visualization exercises include vivid images that are held in the mind that produce healing and comfort. Their repetition creates a learning or conditioning effect, so that the positive physical changes can eventually become available wherever and whenever the person chooses to use them. Imagery often incorporates all the senses, as vividly as possible. Effort is made to actually see, hear, feel, smell, and even taste the imagined scene. How long one focuses on the techniques is usually less important than how regularly they are practiced (a few minutes daily tends to give greater benefits than spending more time less often).

"Today, spend time imagining your life as already healed and happy. Imagine this happy scenario so realistically, that you can feel its reality. When you believe it is so, the physical reality follows."

~ Doreen Virtue

Mind-body techniques work quite well as an adjunct to any conventional or alternative therapy, and can be used along with psychotherapy to more easily facilitate behavioral change. Imagery is also often utilized in conjunction with touch therapies.

"When you visualize then you materialize."

~ Dr. Denis Waitley, Psychologist

The well-known doctor, Andrew Weil, M.D., fully understands the power of the mind-body connection to facilitate physical healing, and actually frequently recommends guided imagery to assist in surgery cases. This has included using imagery CDs both before and after procedures. Additionally, he cites hundreds of studies offering evidence that guided imagery can effectively help decrease pain and the need for pain medication, lower side effects and surgery complications, reduce stress and anxiety before and after procedures, decrease recovery time, increase sleep and immune system health, as well as improve self-confidence and self-control. Dr. Weil's clinical practice has also shown that guided imagery can be quite effective in the treatment of stress-related illnesses, skin problems, and even autoimmunity.

For those who have never tried any type of guided imagery or hypnosis, the idea of getting deeply relaxed and going into a hypnotic trance may seem a bit frightening. However, we all experience trance states in everyday life while daydreaming, watching a movie, driving home on "autopilot", or practicing meditation or other relaxation techniques. Essentially, it is simply an altered state of consciousness. Guided imagery and other forms of hypnosis involve a deliberate choice to enter this state, for a goal often beyond relaxation, which is to focus your concentration and use the power of suggestion in order to promote healing (or reach another goal). A person in trance is always under control, just as someone who is daydreaming can decide to stop at any time. While a practitioner serves as a guide, the only person who can allow the shift in consciousness is you, and trance uncovers the latent potential of your own mind. Therefore, all hypnosis/imagery is truly self-hypnosis/imagery. It is the self-directed aspect that Dr. Weil finds particularly beneficial, as he believes that patients do best when they have understanding and control over their own treatments.

Almost all high-level athletes practice some form of visualization. As author Wayne Dyer said, "You'll see it when you believe it". Spend some time each day visualizing yourself going about your day in a balanced and peaceful manner and watch how your day unfolds in those exact ways! You can include visualization in all of your prayer, meditation, relaxation, acupuncture, and massage therapy sessions.

"Whatever you focus on grows."

~ Maxcia Lizarraga, Couples Counselor

Chapter Thirty-Five

Transform How You Feel About Getting Older

How you feel about aging can become a self-fulfilling prophecy! Therefore it is important to keep your thoughts in-check. Countless studies have actually been done by psychologists, medical doctors, and neuroscientists showing that older people with more negative views of aging fare more poorly on health than those with less pessimistic mindsets. Therefore, how we feel about getting older is proven to be vital to actual outcomes. Researchers are continually finding that if we think about getting older in terms of decline or disability, our health will likely suffer. On the other hand, if we visualize aging in a more positive light, in terms of opportunity and growth, our bodies tend to respond in kind.

Therefore is it clear that we need to be optimistic when seeing our present situations, and in visualizing the future. See a long abundant vibrantly healthy life, full of wisdom, love, happiness, and peace, using affirmations and visualizations that support that positive mind-set, and the body and mind will likely respond in the same manner!

Being successful in this process will definitely have to include being aware and blocking out negative stereotypes about aging that are unfortunately quite pervasive in American society, and re-programming the mind to be more hopeful and positive.

"We do not quit playing because we grow old, we grow old because we quit playing."

~ Oliver Wendell Holmes, Sr.

Chapter Thirty-Six

Mindfulness

Numerous psychotherapists are now using mindfulness techniques in their treatments. It involves focusing completely on the present moment, using all senses, without judgment of any kind. You then become fully present in the moment and notice all that is currently surrounding you.

"BEAUTY surrounds us but do we SEE it?!....... Mindfulness is noticing details in the present moment."

~ Rhonda Hendricks

Mindfulness helps those who have difficulties with the past (affecting present situations), as well as people who are constantly focused on the future (which creates unnecessary stress and fear). Even without the time and place to set up formal practice, from the minute you get up in the morning to the moment you fall asleep at night, there are countless opportunities to engage in mindfulness. It will open you up to better focus, serenity, tranquility, and full enjoyment of life. Really experiencing and taking pleasure in every moment to the fullest will help you savor the times which matter to you the most (for example, precious time with your small child).

"Recognize the beautiful and wonderful things around you, and bless and praise them."

~ Lisa Nichols, Author

I frequently use mindfulness while walking outside, making it a point to focus on all the sights, sounds, aromas, and sensations that I am experiencing. It feels so spiritual and cleansing to me. While I am walking "mindfully" I also keep reminding myself of the present moment, including the date and year I am currently experiencing (adding the time of day), and really take it all in, just in case my mind wants to start wandering into the past or the future! This process also really gives my mind a much-needed time-out.

"See the fullness of life all around you. The warmth of the sun on your skin, the display of magnificent flowers outside the florist's shop, biting into succulent fruit, or getting soaked in the abundance of water falling from the sky. The fullness of life is there at every step. The acknowledgement of that abundance that is all around you awakens the

dormant abundance within. Then let it flow out. When you smile at a

stranger, there is already a minute outflow of energy."

~ Eckhart Tolle

Mindful eating is another approach that many psychotherapists are utilizing now. If you feel you have any "eating issues" I highly recommend you look into mindful eating. It has many benefits!

Along the lines of staying in the present moment, it really helps me to relax and take things "one day at a time", like the Alcoholics Anonymous teachings. Sometimes I even take things "one minute at a time". I tell myself I am doing the best I can, and that my tasks will get done on time. Positive thinking helps me tremendously. Yes, it is still necessary to manage my schedule with my calendar to prevent "over planning", and arrange for what is needed before certain events, but then I put the future out of my mind as much as possible as I go about each day.

Chapter Thirty-Seven

The Benefits of Deep Breathing

Deep breathing exercises can increase the tone of your parasympathetic nervous system, which is the part of the nervous system that promotes relaxation and optimal digestion. These same techniques can actually decrease the tone of your sympathetic nervous system. The sympathetic nervous system's primary process is to stimulate the body's fight-or-flight response.

With a focus on full, cleansing breaths, deep breathing techniques are simple, yet powerful. They are quick and easy to learn, can be practiced almost anywhere, and provide immediate ways to decrease stress levels. Deep breathing is also the foundation of several other relaxation practices (such as those mentioned in this book). Interestingly, I have found it extremely useful with physical symptoms (for example, breathing in and out slowly, completely filling the lungs, can help dissipate pain, tightness, and discomfort around the chest areas). In addition, deep breathing techniques can be combined with other calming elements and movements, such as aromatherapy, relaxation music, and qigong.

Many people are actually breathing incorrectly without even realizing it. For example, if you feel like you are short of breath, are yawning often, or feeling tightness, it could mean there is room for improvement in your breathing. To feel more relaxed, it is helpful for the breath out to be slightly longer than the breath in. Breathing in to the count of five, and out the count of seven, will allow your body to tap into the natural ability to deeply relax. Practicing this several times a day will likely result in thinking more clearly and feeling more calm and content.

There are countless breathing techniques to utilize, therefore I recommend doing some research and incorporate those that feel the most beneficial into your healing activity routines.

DEEP BREATHING MEDITATION EXERCISE EXAMPLES

Belly Breathing Exercise:

Breathe deeply from the abdomen, getting as much fresh air as possible into your body. Taking deep breaths from the abdomen, rather than shallow breaths from the upper chest, allows in more oxygen. The more oxygen you get, the less tense, short of breath, and anxious you will tend to feel. It also is a way to strengthen and increase lower dan tien energy. While breathing, imagine a light shining and flowing into your lower abdomen just below your navel area. Make sure to relax all muscles in that area, which will benefit the entire body.

- Put one hand on your chest and the other on your lower abdomen.

- Inhale deeply (through your nose, or through your mouth like you are breathing through a straw). The hand on your abdomen should rise and the hand on your chest should move very little.

- Exhale (through your nose, or through your mouth like you are breathing through a straw), pushing out as much air as possible while contracting your abdominal muscles. The hand on your abdomen should move in, but your other hand should move very little.

- Continue to breathe in and out, remembering to inhale enough so that your lower abdomen rises and falls, while relaxing all muscles in that area. Slowly exhale, pushing out as much air as possible.

Interestingly, belly breathing is something that most people automatically stop doing as they age. If you get a chance to watch a baby breathe, you will notice that the belly usually rises and falls with each breath, not the chest. Due to stress, anxiety, and tension that tend to build up in life, adults usually breathe into the chest. Belly breathing promotes relaxation and brings a more parasympathetic "rest and digest" state. It loosens up and relaxes abdominal muscles, internal organs, and the lower back, which can help clear out tension and promote digestion.

When we are ill or getting older, breath tends to be weak and shallow. Breathing from the dan tien improves blood circulation, enhances energy and blood, and helps maintain physical as well as mental health. Again, strong healthy energy from the dan tien results in physical health and psychological optimism that aids in preventing depression, dementia, and stagnations in the body. Qigong and Tai Chi are some natural daily activities that can strengthen the dan tien. Doing this can create greater health and enjoyment in life.

The following breathing exercise can help significantly, especially if there is a specific stressor you are trying to neutralize:

Breathe in imagining that with each breath you take your body is filling with relaxation, hope, peace, and positive healing energy. With each exhale imagine you are breathing out all stress, tension, fear, irritation, and frustration. Blow out all the air through your mouth like you are blowing out a candle. Imagine the Universe fully understanding, lovingly absorbing, and taking away all of your stress, tension, fear, irritation, and frustration as you blow out all of the air. During this process, if there are emotions that come to the surface just let them flow out, fully expressing and clearing them without judgment. Continue until the feelings of relaxation, peace, and serenity completely fill your body!

Chapter Thirty-Eight

Gratitude

For me, the most gratitude actually came after the worst hardships. It was when I could lose everything that I truly became the most grateful, even for the simplest things. It is funny how I used to complain and have negative thoughts about tasks such as grocery shopping. Now, after realizing I could have had the potential to lose some functioning in the future due to specific health issues, I am truly grateful to be able to successfully complete each grocery shopping outing! Therefore, my thoughts have changed to positive ones, such as: "I am extremely grateful to be able to complete this shopping trip for myself and my family". Making a gratitude list, referring to it frequently, and using it as part of your daily affirmations can be highly beneficial to overall health.

"A traumatic event shakes you up, and people in that situation have to grab onto positive glimmers of hope; they have to stretch themselves to find a whole new way of living, and that makes their lives more meaningful".

~ Dr. H'Sien Hayward

Every morning upon awakening, think of one thing for which you have gratitude, as this can set the stage for positivity throughout the entire the day. If you can come up with three or more things, even better!

"GRATITUDE. Words Heal. Take a moment to feel "GRATITUDE" in your body, mind and spirit."

~ Nicolas Ortner

Amazingly, gratitude affects the brain at the biological level. Antidepressant medications can boost the neurotransmitters dopamine and serotonin, but so does the daily practice of gratitude. Research shows that feeling grateful activates the brain region that produces dopamine. I have personally observed that grateful people are the happiest. Additionally, cultivating gratitude towards other people increases activity in social dopamine circuits, which makes interactions more enjoyable. Gratitude can also cause positive feedback to circle back and forth in your relationships, therefore express it to your loved ones often. Gratitude is officially linked to positive marital outcomes and can be wonderfully contagious!

Research has been confirming that we can purposely cultivate gratitude and raise our levels of happiness and well-being by doing so. In addition, grateful thinking (especially expression of it to others) is associated with increased levels of energy, optimism, and empathy. The act of increasing gratitude can truly feel magical when you first discover it. It can be an exciting journey, beginning to easily discover blissful treasures from heaven.

"Gratitude is the single most important ingredient to living a successful and fulfilled life."

~ Jack Canfield

Believe me, though, I know there are times life can seem incredibly difficult and it can feel like there is nothing in which to be grateful. You do not have to find something immediately. The searching also counts. But, absolutely as soon as you are able, start with the simple things such as "I have a warm bed to sleep in every night".

Interestingly, I have found that after a while (a few months) of repeating specific affirmations of gratitude, I can now just quickly evoke the feeling of it (without repeating the phrases) and immediately feel the positive effects physically.

"Remember that a grateful heart is a giant magnet for miracles to unfold in your life."

~ Sarah Prout

This chapter would not be complete without including the following quote from my friend Joan, as I definitely could not have said it better myself:

"My wish for you today is that it doesn't take total devastation in your life, as it did me, to appreciate the wonderful miracle of our very existence. To appreciate every day as if this may be our last. To never miss an opportunity to say I love you, to find grace in our lives no matter what struggles we are enduring, and to simply... relish the dance!"

~ Joan Aubele, Author of "The Dance: A Story of Love, Faith, and Survival"

Chapter Thirty-Nine

Other Non-Pharmaceutical Interventions

A few additional effective forms of treatment that do not require medications will be listed and briefly explained in this chapter.

Biofeedback: Another technique I suggest exploring is biofeedback, which has been known to be a natural and effective healing tool for a variety of conditions. Personally, I have only tried it in small amounts, but it was quite helpful. Also I have been told by an autoimmune disease support group leader that biofeedback has helped her tremendously in dealing with the illness. She also stated that she is able to stop her migraines using biofeedback techniques, which was quite interesting. Biofeedback proclaims that people actually have control over many things of which they think they do not have control. For example, you can actually make your hands warmer by thinking your hands are warm and imagining all the blood flowing to your hands. Give it a try!

As a mind-body intervention, biofeedback teaches a person to influence his or her autonomic nervous system, which controls physical functions such as heart rate, blood pressure, brainwaves, and muscle tension. This is done by connecting an electronic "cue" (usually an auditory tone or visual image) to a measurable physiologic process. A person can then monitor his or her internal responses and develop ways to move them in positive healthy directions. Biofeedback machines are sensitive enough to detect internal bodily functions with precision and allow them to be translated in a manner that can be easily understood. The information, or "feedback", that the cue provides is used to monitor functions and facilitate interventions for a variety of conditions, by moving the person toward a more balanced and healthy internal state.

Some conditions known to be effectively treated by biofeedback include:

- Headaches (including migraines)
- Blood pressure issues
- Cardiac arrhythmias
- Urinary incontinence and interstitial cystitis (IC) (also called irritable bladder syndrome)
- Chronic GI conditions such as ulcers, IBS, and Crohn's disease
- Temporomandibular Joint Disorders (TMD/TMJ), and teeth- grinding
- Epilepsy
- Paralysis and other movement disorders
- Hot flashes
- Nausea and vomiting associated with chemotherapy
- Stress and anxiety

Dr. Weil has said research and his experience indicate that biofeedback works best for people whose tension is expressed in bodily complaints such as migraines, hypertension, cardiac arrhythmias, ulcers, chronic intestinal problems, Raynaud's disease, and teeth grinding. It may also benefit those who feel they need outside help in learning to reduce their anxiety and internal stress.

During a typical biofeedback session, the practitioner attaches one or more electrical sensors to parts of the body that yield information about the nervous system and convert it into sound, pictures, color, or a flashing light (something that can be perceived directly). For example, a temperature sensor on a finger can translate skin temperature into a beep tone. The higher the temperature, the faster the beeping. With that kind of feedback, people can actually learn to raise skin temperature and warm their hands. Amazingly, they can consciously relax the sympathetic nervous system that controls the "fight-or-flight response" (constricts blood vessels during high stress). The same pathways can also be used to control changes in the body that accompany any stress-related condition or response, resulting in an improved state of relaxation, balance, and health.

Computerized software and portable devices are available that can provide biofeedback with little training. It can be learned by self-instruction via computer. Electrical sensors usually detect changes in pulse or heart rate variability and offer feedback by way of audio or visual cues, some even in the form of a game experience. In addition, companies that use portable computerized biofeedback equipment usually offer training programs for professionals who can teach clients how to use the technology. Therefore, biofeedback is especially advantageous since it can be practiced with little need for training, or self-taught with minimal guidance (via listening to a CD, DVD, app, or computer program).

Biofeedback, like other mind-body techniques, can be used quite effectively along with other therapies that help induce the relaxation response. Acupuncture, massage, and other touch therapies can all work together, accomplishing even more than they could alone.

Like all relaxation techniques, biofeedback can balance cortisol levels, which can stabilize insulin and affect blood sugar in a healthy way. According to the Mayo Clinic, diabetics should discuss this treatment option with their doctors, however keep a careful watch over their blood sugar if they use biofeedback for a long period of time (it may interfere with other diabetes treatments). It is not recommended for those with major mental health conditions or during an acute psychiatric emergency. Otherwise, biofeedback is considered safe.

Ortho-Bionomy: Aiming to help people break the cycle of pain, Ortho-Bionomy, is a gentle form of body therapy that works with the nervous system and eases chronic pain, stress, post-trauma difficulties, injuries, and more. Find additional information and practitioner listings at: www.ortho-bionomy.org.

Transcranial Magnetic Stimulation: A safe and proven non-drug, non-invasive, therapy option for depression is Transcranial Magnetic Stimulation (TMS). It is a procedure that uses magnetic fields to stimulate nerve cells in the brain to decrease symptoms.

While the patient reclines in a chair, a TMS magnet is gently placed on his or her head sending magnetic pulses to areas of the brain associated with depression. It painlessly delivers a magnetic pulse that stimulates nerve cells in the brain region connected with moods, which helps to activate areas of the brain that are known to have decreased activity in those with depression.

Patients can resume their regular routines and activities immediately following TMS procedures. It is safe with none of the side effects associated with most anti-depressant medications or electroconvulsive therapy (ECT) as there is no sexual dysfunction, weight gain, sedation, or memory loss. The treatment is applied externally to a specific area and does not enter the rest of the body. This safety and efficacy make it possible to be referred to TMS even if you have tried only one pharmaceutical and it has not worked.

Unfortunately, excessive amounts of people struggle with depression and often are on too many synthetic medications, in my opinion. TMS can be a beneficial treatment option for patients who are not satisfied with pharmaceuticals. TMS is also currently covered by a few health insurance plans and is something to explore if you are experiencing significant depression. The FDA has also just approved TMS to treat obsessive compulsive disorder (OCD).

Light Box for Depression: Light boxes are another effective non-pharmaceutical treatment option for a type of depression called Seasonal Affective Disorder (SAD). Countless people have found that after one winter using it they will never go without it again! Some also use light boxes throughout the summer as well. Additionally, there is new evidence that light boxes work for other types of depression. There are studies finding it beneficial for jet lag recovery as well. Interestingly, light boxes are being used to ease the "sundowning" that is seen in Alzheimer's.

It is important to work with your healthcare provider before purchasing a light box, and to receive education on how to use it correctly (and understand any possible associated risks in your specific case). Use with a bit of caution, as it is possible for a manic episode to be stimulated with some patients who are prone to bipolar type depression. It can also cause insomnia in some people if used too close to bedtime. Keep in mind that light boxes must be used consistently, as the benefits may drop off after non-use. But, it is such a simple, non-invasive, natural treatment method that can work extremely well if used correctly and monitored appropriately.

At the time of this writing, "The Sunbox Company" comes highly recommended by my mental health professional colleagues as a one of the top places to obtain high-quality light boxes, and the customer service is outstanding. Check out their website: sunbox.com.

Chapter Forty

Hair and Scalp Health

If you are experiencing any type of hair loss or hair health concerns, I surely know how it can feel. Nutrition issues, stress, medical conditions, imbalances, genetics, pharmaceuticals, and personal care products can all significantly affect overall hair health, growth, and loss.

Plenty of natural holistic health interventions are provided in this book and working on those activities will most likely reduce hair loss issues in many cases. However, there are <u>three top suggestions</u> I will give along those lines.

- The first is to find ways to love and accept yourself, while working to calm your mind and body down (including continually expressing deep gratitude for any hair you currently still have).
- The second suggestion is to focus as much as you can on positive and optimistic thoughts about the future.
- The third is to make sure you are getting enough nutrients through your diet. Biotin, in particular, seems to be of high importance to hair

health. Additional supplementation may be needed which is something to research for yourself, working with your healthcare provider. Use some caution with biotin supplementation if there are any thyroid issues.

Because every case is so different in regards to hair loss, feel free to also email us at our confidential email address (gs@ginaspielman.com) with your story. Include the important highlights and we can fill in any other information by asking any additional necessary questions. We can then begin to set up a helpful plan along with you, given your specific health condition and situation.

"I lovingly groom my hair and choose the thoughts that support its growth and strength. I love and appreciate my beautiful hair!"

~ Louise Hay

Chapter Forty-One

Oral Hygiene Affects Overall Health

Keep in mind that oral hygiene is extremely important to overall health. If you see a holistic doctor who is thorough, he or she will ask about your teeth and gums, as well as your oral hygiene. Be sure to brush and floss your teeth regularly, as directed by your dental health professional. Regular brushing and flossing reduces the amount of potentially harmful bacteria that can enter your body, which then supports overall health. It appears that bacteria in the mouth may cause inflammation throughout the body. We know that if you have moderate to advanced gum disease, harmful oral bacteria can enter your bloodstream (Dental News & Views, Vol. 25, Issue 10). Brushing and flossing regularly also helps to prevent major dental procedures from having to be done (procedures which can take a toll mentally and physically, not to mention financially). In addition, some studies have shown that flossing once a day increases a person's life expectancy by six years. If you do not already have enough incentive to take good care of your mouth, teeth, and gums, the connection between your oral and overall health provides even more. Make a promise to yourself to practice excellent oral hygiene daily as you are making an investment in your health, not just for now, but for the future. Also, be sure to keep all your dental cleaning visit appointments!

The oral use of coconut oil has been shown to be beneficial to the health of the teeth and gums. Coconut oil is an anti-microbial agent, due, in part, to its lauric acid content. Also, coconut oil produces a soap-like substance when the saliva mixes with the oil (saponification). Soaps produced with coconut oil can lather well and have increased cleansing action. The lauric acid in the coconut oil reacts with sodium hydroxide in saliva to form sodium laureate (the main constituent of soap), which is probably responsible for the cleansing action as well as decreased plaque accumulation. You will have to research the exact method, but swishing your mouth out with coconut oil (do not gargle) may be more effective, and safer, than chemical mouthwash. There is also a way to make an inexpensive, natural, and effective toothpaste using coconut oil, and is also something worth researching.

If you tend to get blisters on your lips, inner cheeks, or gums, look into using witch hazel to speed up healing and eliminate pain and swelling. Certain witch hazel extracts can be applied to the inside of the mouth to decrease bleeding, blisters, sores, odors, and infections of the gums, especially when combined with other healing oils like coconut or peppermint.

Drinking green tea can naturally improve the health of your gums and teeth, as it helps decrease inflammation, makes your mouth more alkaline, inhibits the growth of cavity-causing bacteria, destroys odor-causing bacteria, helps prevent tooth loss, and may slow progression of oral cancer (remember though that green tea does contain some caffeine, and it is not for everyone).

Warm salt water can also be used as a mouthwash or gargle occasionally. I am a fan of salt water gargle when one is ill with a cold. Peroxide as a mouthwash can also help gums heal and keep them healthy, but do not do this more than once per day, and make sure you follow the directions on the container. Consult your dental professional first before you try peroxide mouthwash.

Chapter Forty-Two

Live Blood Analysis and "The Blood Type Diet®"

Obtaining all the test results possible will facilitate placing all of your "puzzle" pieces together, especially if you are still not feeling 100% and you do not know all of the underlying causes of your condition(s). Along those lines, I was referred by my former acupuncturist to see a nurse who does live blood analyses. Upon her review, my blood report and pictures actually ended up looking pretty good. All the positive healing activities that I had been doing were evident in my blood. She could tell I had been consuming a large number of vegetables on a daily basis and said I was doing incredibly well with that aspect. This information encouraged me to eat even more vegetables! She agreed that I was "on the mend" physically and just need the few added changes. We also spoke about the importance of tending to mental health and how it all affects the physical body, such as keeping cortisol levels lower. "Visualization of health" is also imperative.

Conditions she could see in live blood apparently included leaky gut, adrenal concerns, difficulty processing protein, and blood sugar issues. In addition, because she could see "food sensitivities" in blood, she highly recommended following "The Blood Type Diet®" (and therefore I made some additional dietary changes). Healing gut issues is a priority for the completion of health restoration, and eating the right foods for one's particular body is an important part of that goal. There was a general message that disease begins in the gut and that is where it can be healed as well. Interestingly, bananas were referred to as the biggest "no-no" food for my "A" blood type and I was eating at least one per day. She said that just cutting those out of my diet would help tremendously! It seems that those with type "A" blood tend to have more sensitive constitutions and are more prone to diseases. Too much stress on their bodies from certain foods, medications, chemicals, hormones, and lifestyle issues often weakens the health of their immune systems more quickly than with other blood types. For all blood types, following "The Blood Type Diet®" can aid in the process of fending off viruses as well as weight loss.

She advocated the use of digestive enzyme supplements (she also said that vegetables have enzymes), as well as aloe for faster gut healing. Live blood can also show a problem with cortisol and there was an additional supplement available for that as well. She could also see skin problems reflected in blood, as well as a lack of nutrients such as B vitamins, magnesium, and iron. In addition, she had the ability to see past vaccines and antibiotic use. Amazingly, blood can also indicate if someone has been in a "fight-or-flight" mode, even since birth. What makes the body go into that mode are situations such as severe emotional stress as well as food sensitivities (for example giving a baby who should be avoiding milk a milk-based formula for a long period of time).

Levels of yeast could also apparently be seen in blood, as well as heavy metals. According to her, some yeast is actually necessary to have in the GI tract, as it assists with digestion. She saw a small amount of heavy metals in my blood, but not what she would consider "heavy metal toxicity". She also had the ability to see liver issues as well as viruses (including dormant ones).

Interestingly, she could see if one's system had been overwhelmed over time. When a body is in that state it can get to a point where it cannot handle anything additional very well, such as any new stress, poor diet, allergens, chemicals, or any "bugs" that want to get in and take over. That could surely explain the odd immune response that I am sure many of you have experienced.

Another interesting topic we touched upon was that she clearly stated that the Paleo diet (which I had been considering for quite some time, and trying on and off) would not be beneficial for me. The Paleo diet, in the traditional sense, probably would have made my health decline. I am thinking this is mostly due to the difficulty processing protein, how red and some other types of meat do not "fit" well with my blood type, and how coconut products, which are so widely used in Paleo diets, are an "avoid" food for my blood type. At the time of this writing it does not appear that I need to go completely grain free. That may change in the future but it seems to be working well with including some gluten free grains. I do appreciate, however, many Paleo dessert products and tend to do pretty well with those as an occasional treat.

Chapter Forty-Three

Leaky Gut

Leaky gut syndrome is not yet acknowledged by most Western medical doctors at the time of this writing, but evidence is mounting that it is a legitimate condition that involves the intestinal lining. Leaky gut syndrome (also called increased intestinal permeability), is said to be the result of damage to the intestinal lining, making it less able to protect the internal environment as well as to filter essential nutrients and other substances. Bacteria, toxins, yeast, viruses, incompletely digested proteins and fats, and waste not normally absorbed, can then leak out of the intestines into the blood stream. This then triggers an autoimmune reaction, which can lead to GI problems (such as abdominal bloating, excessive gas, and cramping), food sensitivities, fatigue, joint discomfort, skin rashes, and autoimmunity. Some conditions and activities that are said to lead to leaky gut syndrome are chronic inflammation, food sensitivities, compromised immunity, damage from taking large amounts of non-steroid anti-inflammatory drugs (NSAIDS), cytotoxic drugs, radiation, taking certain antibiotics, and excessive alcohol consumption.

Leaky gut syndrome may trigger or worsen bowel conditions (including Crohn's disease, IBS, or celiac disease), RA, and asthma, and you probably have leaky gut syndrome if you have any of those conditions. Some also say that all people with any type of autoimmune disease have leaky gut. I tend to agree that healing gut issues also helps sufferers of mental health issues as well. But, as with many issues, I often think "What came first, the chicken or the egg" because I am definitely more happy and content when I am not having tummy issues! Nonetheless, it is proven that having gut health helps overall health, no matter how you look at it. Who knows how many other countless conditions would be aided by healing the gut!

Treatment of leaky gut syndrome includes an assortment of dietary supplements and healthy lifestyle changes (included in this book). There are certain foods and beverages which can help repair the intestines, and there are ones to avoid. In addition, following "The Blood Type Diet®" as much as possible is something I highly recommend in order to assist in healing the gut and entire immune system, and enhance overall health.

"The leaky gut treatment I recommend involves avoiding alcohol and NSAIDS as well as any foods that you're allergic to. Make sure you're eating plenty of fiber. Take Culturelle or another probiotic supplement containing Lactobacillus GG. I would also recommend eating an anti-inflammatory diet, including essential fatty acids like fish oil and GLA. In addition, you might try supplementing with glutamine, an amino acid that helps maintain intestinal metabolism and function and seems to

benefit patients who have had intestinal injury from chemotherapy and
radiation. "

~ **Andrew Weil, M.D.**

I have personally found the following nutritional smoothie mix to be extremely helpful in restoring gut health as well as aiding in the detoxification process: MediClear Plus® by Thorne Research® (available online). This is a supplement to use just for shorter periods of time, not on an ongoing basis. There has also been a special diet associated with the smoothie mix, designed to help with detoxification, decreasing inflammation, healing gut issues, and decreasing allergies.

"Chris Kehler Holistic" is another consideration to assist in leaky gut healing. Chris is an Energy/Bio-Spiritual Healer. Again, he has called himself "The Alternative to the Alternative". Check out his website: ChrisKehler.net. If the information resonates with you, consider making an appointment.

- Also see the "Bone Broth" chapter for more on leaky gut healing.

Chapter Forty-Four

Natural Hormone Balancing

Naturally balancing your hormones can increase physical as well as emotional health. Stabilizing your hormones will often relieve PMS, cramps, headaches, bloating, depression, and so much more.

As far as autoimmune goes, it is quite interesting that many more women than men are getting diagnosed with autoimmune diseases. Of the fifty million (or more) Americans living and coping with autoimmune conditions, more than seventy five percent of them are women. Therefore, autoimmune diseases seem to be striking women three times more than men. Some specific diagnoses have an even higher incidence in women. Of course, there are many potential third variables (other reasons why there are more women than men), but one important factor could be hormones. On a side note there are other theories such as women being less likely to deal with anger in healthy ways, therefore creating imbalance in the body. Nonetheless, more research needs to be done, but we do know that stabilizing hormones with diet, exercise, and other activities will likely help to decrease autoimmune symptoms. Getting the body back into complete balance is the path to vibrant health. The "hormone theory" for autoimmunity also gives another reason for women to look forward to post-menopause (the other being lack of menstruation!), as some autoimmune symptoms could subside after menopause.

In general, maintaining an excellent diet (and following many of the suggestions in this book) will help you naturally maintain more balanced hormone levels, but there are some specific additional dietary changes that can further improve them. There are also lifestyle adjustments and treatments that can help you naturally get back into balance as well. Some of these include:

- Eat foods high in Omega-3 fatty acids. Omega-3 creates healthy cell membranes, allowing hormones to reach their destinations within the body. Some foods to consider including are fish (such as wild salmon, Atlantic mackerel, anchovies, lake trout, herring, and sardines), raw walnuts, chia seeds, flaxseeds, and certain types of eggs.

- Increase fiber. Fruits and vegetables are excellent examples of high fiber sources. Fiber binds itself to old estrogen, helping to clear it out of the body, leading to better overall hormone balance.

- Zinc is known to aid in the production of testosterone. Foods high in zinc include high quality dark chocolate, peanuts, and meats (including beef, veal, lamb, crab, and oysters).

- Probiotics also help to balance hormones in the body. It seems like every day we learn another new way the microflora in our gut dramatically influences our health. I think anyone who is not regularly ingesting "good bacteria" could be missing out on one of the best opportunities available to increase overall health.

- Avocados have hormone-balancing properties.

- Coconut products (such as a bit of high-quality coconut oil) can also help to balance hormones.

- Roman Chamomile essential oil is used to help stabilize hormones.

- If you eat animal products, choose high-quality brands that have no hormones added.

- Avoid caffeine and alcohol. Studies show that excessive use of either one contributes to premenstrual hormonal imbalance.

- Get more sleep and decrease stress. Remember that stress and a lack of sleep may cause some glands to malfunction.

- Participate in mild to moderate exercise on a daily basis.

- Chiropractic adjustments and Chinese medicine/acupuncture treatments can also help to naturally balance hormones.

Be careful with plastic! Chemicals in plastics may interfere with hormones (they can contain hormone disrupting chemicals) as well as introduce more toxins into the body. Do not microwave with plastic containers, place plastic wrap onto hot food, or leave full drinking water bottles in a hot car. Pay attention to your pots, pans, bowls, and utensils used for cooking. Use stainless steel and cast iron pots and utensils as much as possible (a side-bonus from cooking with cast iron is that it can increase your iron level if used consistently). Also along the lines of avoiding plastic, glass and ceramic are usually fine to use in cooking and food storage. Avoid non-stick plastic-coated surfaces in any of your cooking whenever possible. Heat can make the chemicals leach into the food or liquid more easily. When you absolutely have to use a plastic product, choose "BPA Free" whenever possible as that is likely a better option (although more research needs to be done on that topic).

Chapter Forty-Five

Eat Well

A healthy diet provides the essential building blocks for neurotransmitters and physical health. Therefore, it is imperative to eat the best diet you possibly can.

"The problem is that calories are cheap. Nutrition is expensive."

~ Tom Colicchio, Chef and Television Personality

Most people are confused about what to eat, especially if diagnosed with an illness, such as an autoimmune disease. I encourage you to listen to your body, first and foremost, and make more loving food choices. I have found that properly nourishing my body makes doing the affirmations, keeping good moods, and making other healthy choices much easier.

As said previously, I follow what is called "The Blood Type Diet®" as much as possible. You can find information about this diet on: www.dadamo.com (Official Website of Dr. Peter J. D'Adamo & The Blood Type Diet®). Taking every opportunity to follow the diet that is right for your blood type can assist you greatly in the road back to health. I really love knowing the foods that are therapeutic for me and therefore I fill up on those items (such as carrots) every chance I get.

If you are trying to restore your health, I suggest avoiding sugar (especially refined processed sugars). When sugar is refined, it is usually stripped of anything beneficial. The sugar then becomes difficult for the body to process. The body must release large amounts of nutrients to convert sugar into energy, which in turn causes acid formation. Some say sugar could be considered an "anti-nutrient" as it can rob the body of nutrients. Also many fruit juices, dried fruits, and some fresh fruits that are rich in fructose should be consumed relatively sparingly due to the high "sugar" content (but at least they have nutrients and other benefits). Try to drink whole fruit smoothies instead of juices (maintaining the fiber helps to lower blood sugar spikes, and you can also add even more fiber to smoothies with ingredients such as psyllium husk powder). Also avoid highly processed food as it can contribute to inflammation in many people. Minimize simple carbohydrates as they usually give only temporary "energy" and can lead to more uneven blood sugar levels (which can cause a number of health and wellbeing issues). Complex carbohydrates are better because they usually provide more nutrients and fiber, and longer-standing (more balanced) energy. Try to limit products containing white flour from grains. For sweeteners try a bit of Stevia in the Raw® (large bags, in baking aisle of most grocery stores; personally, I think this type has the best taste), pure maple syrup (watered down if using on waffles or pancakes), or natural raw honey (I am a fan of Manuka honey). Be sure to still use all the natural sweeteners sparingly. Ideally, training yourself to decrease your desire for "sweet" tastes and starchy foods will be best for your health. You will be surprised what you begin getting used to (such as much lower sugar), and how much this can benefit any medical, mental health, or addiction issues. Research the possibility of adding chromium as a supplement to help control cravings and regulate blood sugar levels.

Also consider going dairy-free and gluten-free, especially if you have any digestive issues or inflammation. If you eat pasta or noodles, try gluten free versions. I have enjoyed lentil pasta purchased online. It is quite high in nutrients and fiber, and because of its protein content, it can also be used as a meat substitute. Pastas made with brown rice and rice bran have been a favorite of mine as well. Note that cooking gluten free pasta is a bit touchy and can be somewhat of a learning curve to get it just right for you. Be patient and keep trying! Eating gluten free is getting much easier as time goes on. For just one example, there are countless restaurants that do GF quite well now.

Eat all-natural and buy organic whenever possible. Organic is non-GMO and much more. Try to eat foods which have not been genetically modified. Be careful of highly processed soy products, or too much corn (especially the non-organic types).

Try to avoid microwaving your food, as much as you possibly can. As an example, I have begun cooking carrots on the stovetop instead of in the microwave. It really is just as fast, the amount of dishes to wash ends up the same, and the result is a far superior product. There are also ways frozen vegetables can be baked, therefore keep your mind open to new ideas and recipes.

Drink most of your fluids in between meals. Do not flood a meal by drinking too many liquids (especially cold drinks), as that could interfere with digestion and absorption.

You can lower your salt intake by using substitutes for what you have been eating. For example, you can change to unsalted nuts, or add fresh vegetables to already salted foods in a meal in order to balance out the salt content. You can also use certain herbs and spices to add flavor. Sea or rock salts are typically better for your body than the "common" refined highly processed salt that has been stripped of its nutrients. In our house we use Himalayan pink salt in place of "common" salt. I have recently seen it in my local grocery store spice section as well as at local spice shops. Make sure your Himalayan pink salt comes from a trusted source.

Himalayan pink salt is whole unprocessed natural salt which contains minerals. It is best when consumed with high-quality spring water. Some of the benefits of using this salt in place of "common" salt are said to include:

- Creating an electrolyte balance and increasing hydration
- Regulating water content both inside and outside of cells
- Balancing pH (alkaline/acidity) and reducing acid reflux
- Helping the intestines absorb nutrients
- Aiding in proper metabolism functioning
- Strengthening bones
- Helping to reduce the signs of aging
- Preventing goiters
- Improving circulation and preventing muscle cramping
- Supporting respiratory and sinus health
- Helping to detoxify the body from substances such as heavy metals
- Supporting libido
- Regulating and naturally promoting sleep
- Supporting healthy blood sugar levels
- Helping blood pressure (especially when taken with spring water)

That said, even though Himalayan pink salt is typically considered a healthier salt, there are some conditions which may require a low or no salt diet. Please follow all necessary medical recommendations for your particular condition.

If you are able, you will have to familiarize yourself with everything in health food stores and natural health aisles, as well as understand you will be making frequent shopping trips for fresh produce (or have them delivered).

"Eat food. Not too much. Mostly plants."

~ Michael Pollan

Lately, I have been reading that eating raw vegetables (such as celery) decreases inflammation in the body. Therefore, I highly recommend keeping a bag of "ready-to-eat" raw veggies in the fridge to munch on whenever you feel hungry, instead of reaching for the junk food! Recently, I have found sugar snap peas to be a delicious, easy, and satisfying snack.

Personally, I have also found that healthy nuts or seeds can satisfy hunger quite well. For example, my "Nuts.com" raw organic walnuts are good for my health and also help prevent me from reaching for a bag of chips!

"The problem is we are not eating food any more, we are eating food-like products."

~ Dr Alejandro Junger

Think of food being positive energy, and for your health, first and foremost. Having thoughts such as "there is an abundance of nourishment" will also help mind, body, and spirit. Eat a well-balanced diet which consists of a high amount of different vegetables, fruits, nuts, seeds, herbs, and spices (all as tolerated of course). This way you will be sure to get the benefits of each "superfood", which there are many (avocados, blueberries, walnuts, asparagus, beets, kale, and countless more).

There is also new research out which suggests that having acidic blood can create illness or cause the body to be unable to heal. Therefore the pH level of the blood could be extremely important. The research states that alkaline blood is ideal and promotes health (prevents illness and aids healing). Therefore, I suggest looking into what is called "the alkaline diet" in order to receive more information (make sure it is from a trusted source because there seems to be conflicting information on the internet). A few of the most alkaline foods are said to be: carrots, broccoli, kale, and chamomile tea. These are also among the top healing foods for my "A" blood type. Therefore I am consuming as many of those as possible. My sister had informed me about the naturally alkaline spring water "Eternal" which I purchase at my local grocery store. As a side note about pH levels in the body: chronic emotional stress can also cause the body to become more acidic.

Some people absolutely swear by the Paleo diet, some say the raw diet is best, and some others say vegan is the only way to go. I have also heard that eating all non-genetically modified foods has significantly helped many who have suffered autoimmune diseases. The alkaline diet is getting a significant amount of attention as well, and so are the Ketogenic Diet and the Mediterranean Diet (the Mediterranean Diet is relatively easy to follow). I believe there are many positives to each approach, but there are also some negatives in my opinion. Again, the "The Blood Type Diet®" has worked wonders for me and I urge you to follow it as much as you possibly can during your healing, in addition to making other changes you find are important for your particular body along the way.

"Each meal is a chance to heal."

~ Mark Hyman, M.D.

I am not going to tell you what healthy eating plans will work best for your particular body and health condition(s), but you owe it to yourself to do everything you can to figure out which ones will be the most healing. For just one example, there is emerging evidence that following the Ketogenic Diet is highly beneficial for cancer cases. Now, I am not going to say to "forget the chemo and just do the special diet". However, the special diet could augment the chemotherapy and likely help to enhance its effectiveness; therefore it is something to definitely research if cancer is one of your concerns. Also, if you happen to be one of those cases where Western medicine is stating nothing can be done for the cancer, then as you take your "outside steps" (stepping outside the Western medical model), by all means the Ketogenic Diet is absolutely a promising option to research (along with implementing several other suggestions in this book).

Many have been helped by what is called the Specific Carbohydrate Diet. There is a book available, as well as a website which contains the diet information, recipes, and a significant amount of education on how to heal autoimmune and severe gut issues (such as Crohn's): www.scdlifestyle.com. There is also the "Low FODMAP Diet Approach: Eliminating many of the

Dietary Triggers for the symptoms of IBS". The aim of this plan is relief from IBS and, in some cases, inflammatory bowel disease. Many have been helped by following the Low FODMAP Diet Approach, and I know that some medical doctors actually recommend it as well, therefore it is worth researching. I do want to say, however, that if you are having any type of intestinal inflammation (symptoms such as bloating, gas, diarrhea, constipation, pain, or discomfort) the three top foods to avoid are dairy, gluten, and refined processed sugar, in my opinion. If you begin with eliminating those three, along with eating a natural well-balanced diet, I think you will have relief quite quickly. Then of course you will also have to avoid anything in which you are allergic or intolerant. Also limit any food or substance that causes you GI distress. In addition, following the suggestions in the 'Anti-Inflammatory Foods" chapter under "foods and substances to avoid" section (reducing inflammation) will also likely help, along with many of my other lifestyle recommendations. As far as excessive gas and bloating go, some natural doctors recommend not eating fruits with other foods. If you have a high amount of gas and bloating, and you feel like you have tried everything, then start only eating fruit before or well after other foods and meals. Therefore, try not eating fruit with or right after meals and see if that helps your situation.

Along these lines of proper digestion, Maged Rizk, MD, Gastroenterologist at Cleveland Clinic, has said that all medications need to be reviewed with your doctor, since drugs like antidepressants, antacids, antihistamines, pain relievers, and blood pressure medications might all affect digestion.

Remember to eat slowly, chewing your food completely. Unfortunately, Americans are well known for eating way too fast, and frequently "on the run". Do not rush through your meals, sit at a table while eating, and relax during and after meals. Digestion begins in the mouth and you have all the power to give it a great start! Allowing your body to properly digest food supports the immune system, reduces after-meal fatigue, and enables your endocrine system to process nutrition at an optimal level. Avoid large meals, especially before bedtime, in order to ensure proper digestion. Use positive affirmations while preparing food and while eating, such as "This glorious food is healthy for me", "It provides vibrant energy for me and my family", "I am grateful to have this nourishment", "I am absorbing all of the nutrients", and "I am digesting the food well and at a healthy pace". Amazingly, this can create positive energy for yourself and your family (physically, mentally, and spiritually). It can also actually put positive energy into the food! Studies have been done using special photography proving this phenomenon. As long as you know you are doing your best with what you have on your plate, having a "higher vibration" while cooking and eating can also greatly reduce "food fear", which will be beneficial to health.

"Staying in a state where we keep our vibrations high affects everything around us including the food we eat."

~ Sandra Ingerman, MA

I would say there are three reasons to try not to eat the exact same things every single day. One is that you will be less likely to create new food allergies. Second is that if you are sensitive to a food, and you are unaware of it (sometimes allergies are a delayed response and therefore difficult to detect), then if you are not eating that food every single day there will be less impact on your system. Third is receiving a wider array of nutrients and benefits because you can vary your diet with even more superfoods (those which contain natural ingredients to ward off disease and infection). To help decrease food allergies and its effects on the body, some alternative healthcare providers recommend what is called a "rotation diet", which is definitely something to consider. Another way some health-conscious people "rotate" their diets is to eat seasonally (only what is "in season" at the time). Therefore, just be sure to take some breaks from your routine foods from time to time.

Different types of fasting have proven to have various health benefits. Brief intermittent fasting periods can be therapeutic for the body and is definitely something to research, in my opinion. Also, many have been helped by going on juice fasts, which means juicing fresh veggies and fruits and consuming only that for a period of time. Please review with your health professional prior to going on a juice fast, and I recommend juicing mostly veggies and not so many fruits due to the high "sugar" (and low fiber) content of fruit juices.

Open your mind to eating certain foods at different times of the day, as well as new combinations. For example, I have started eating carrots first thing in the morning. You can also eat snacks such as almond and flaxseed pancakes during the day. In addition, consider having "mini meals" (leftover from your main meals) for snacks. Eggs are included in some "dinner" recipes as well. There are really no rules as to what time and for what meal everyone should be eating certain foods, and what combinations you can try. Also open your mind to including healthy foods or flavorings to your routine meals, such as adding raw walnuts and Ceylon cinnamon to your morning cereal.

Managing your diet may seem time-consuming at first, but all of the benefits it offers makes it well worth it! For just one example (among countless others), it is a known fact that most fibromyalgia sufferers find relief through a properly managed diet. You will need to understand and accept the fact that more time will be spent on meal planning, shopping, cooking, and enjoying food. This is how the Italians have always done it, and they would not have it any other way! Therefore, open your mind to a new way of being in regards to eating.

I recommend compiling a list of healthy recipes (meals, snacks, baked goods, and beverages). Seek out recipes that have the potential to help heal disease instead of contributing to it.

Chapter Forty-Six

Detoxify the Body

Detoxifying your body is essential to decreasing inflammation and improving overall health. The main elimination systems are the liver, kidneys, bowels, lungs, lymph, and skin (including underarm areas). Interestingly, the lungs actually release toxins through breathing. The job of the liver is to cleanse the blood of toxins and work with the bowels and kidneys to eliminate anything unnecessary from the body. The kidneys also remove toxins from the blood while assisting in the excretion of excess water through urine. The lymphatic system collects cellular waste, dead red blood cells, white blood cells filled with debris, and chemicals from bodily tissues, and then passes them to the eliminatory systems for excretion. The lymphatic system works with the liver, kidneys, bowels, lungs, and skin. If one system is blocked or does not work correctly, it all falls on the others to do the work and can result in health issues.

Reflecting on my past, I can see that toxins have played a role in developing illness. The absolute first thing I needed to do in order to detoxify was to lighten up my toxin load. I knew that would begin calming down my immune system, as well as reduce sensitivity issues and inflammation. If you have a serious health condition, it is important to avoid alcohol, cigarette smoke, and refined processed sugars, all of which act as toxins in the body and are obstacles to your healing process (coffee/caffeine and certain "bad" fats are also probably on that list, and should be minimized, in my opinion). Stay away from chemicals whenever possible! You can start by decreasing the use of chemical-based household cleaners and personal health care products (cleansers, shampoos, soaps, deodorants, make-up, lotions, and toothpastes), and substitute with natural alternatives. Also, always wear protective gear while cleaning, especially if you are using anything containing chemicals.

In addition, you may want to do some research and install a water filter or water conditioner in your home, to help remove toxins and anything else undesirable (this also can benefit your hair follicles according to my holistic hair stylist). There are also shower nozzle attachments available. In addition, some filters can be geared towards the kitchen water use only. As a side note here, it is a good idea to make sure the majority of your drinking water is more on the alkaline side as opposed to acidic, as that seems to be the best for most health conditions (alkaline filters do exist if that is needed). Water conditioning companies usually do free water analyses so you can look into that as well (make sure it is from a highly experienced reputable organization). If you are within your city limits, familiarize yourself with your city's water analysis reports.

Having fresh air inside your home is necessary for optimal health. Open windows whenever you can. Even if it is winter, if the weather is mild and sunny you can crack a window and get some air circulation. Not only does it boost your mood, but there are toxins and such inside our homes and there is no possible way to remove them all, therefore it is highly beneficial to get some air flow. Fill your lungs with fresh air even if it is cold outside. Breathing deeply will allow oxygen to circulate more completely throughout your system. This only takes seconds and it will remind you that you are alive and breathing! If you live in a polluted area, have environmental allergies, or there are problems with your indoor air quality, I highly recommend getting an air cleaner for your home.

Throughout our house we have natural air "purifying" Himalayan salt lamp lights. They are said to produce negative ions (beneficial to the human body), and this creates a healthy environment similar to when you are near an outside stream or waterfall. The lamps also provide a calming and relaxing beautiful glow in the room. Make sure you purchase your Himalayan salt lamps from trusted sources.

I absolutely need to emphasize the importance of using only all natural non-toxic air fresheners, neutralizers, odor absorbers, and essential oil diffusers in your home and office. Some high quality essential oils are said to actually purify the air. Interestingly, certain houseplants are used to increase indoor air quality as well, by helping to lower toxins. In addition, there are effective non-toxic "insecticides" available. One is called Diatomaceous Earth (DE), and in addition to being used around your home it is "food grade" and seems to have numerous health promoting benefits when used as a supplement.

"Breathing in, I calm my body. Breathing out, I smile. Dwelling in the present moment, I know this is a wonderful moment."

~ Thich Nhat Hanh

To further decrease your toxin load, I suggest finding a "holistic" hair stylist, if you have not done so already. My stylist (whose services are called "Holistic Hair by Trish") uses effective hair treatments that are not so toxic (more natural) and works in a small private salon. Therefore, while getting my hair done I am not breathing in so many toxins from all the caustic hair treatments and styling products that are present in large salons. She also has methods of detoxifying and clearing out hair follicles so that more hair is free to grow. Having her services available so close to home is truly a blessing! I urge you to seek out a similar situation in your area. There are other natural "at-home" ways to color hair as well. Look into all of your options!

- See "Natural Hormone Balancing" chapter for information on avoiding plastics in order to decrease your toxin load.

When doing any home decorating or remodeling, use more eco-friendly products. It is possible to complete home improvement projects and keep toxins and odors to a minimum.

Another deterrent to good health, and increase in toxin load, is negative stress. Stress triggers the body to release certain hormones. While these hormones can provide the "adrenaline rush" to win a race or meet a deadline, large amounts of negative stress creates toxins and slows down detoxification enzymes in the liver. "Negative" emotions must be released from the body as well, or they will cause problems. Yoga, qigong, and meditation are simple and effective ways to calm down your mental and physical stress reactions. There are also loads of other activities recommended in this book that help in stress reduction. Just remember to emphasize and focus on positive emotions whenever possible!

I am sure you have noticed that there are countless detoxification programs and supplements available. Work with your healthcare provider to determine the best course of action for your particular detoxification or liver cleanse needs. The specific program or plan you chose may depend on what you are trying to rid your body from, and what you need to avoid might depend on your specific "toxicity", such as aluminum in some cases. From what I have read and from my experience, the best preliminary plan might be to do a liver detoxification. A liver cleanse regime at least once per year will likely eliminate any foreign substances trapped in your liver. I also recommend getting tested for heavy metal toxicity as mercury and other metals can cause autoimmunity and other issues. Again, I urge you to work with your healthcare professional to decide which detoxification program would be best for you (and also to determine if you are able to complete an actual program in the first place).

There is basic program created by Dr. Oz which is only 48 hours long and contains numerous extremely healthy foods, herbs, and spices. It claims to "revitalize you from the inside out" and from the ingredient list, it looks like it could do the trick! There is a website that contains all the instructions and shopping list: www.doctoroz.com/article/48-hour-weekend-cleanse.

You can also cleanse your body daily, following these diet, supplement, and lifestyle practices:

1. Consume plenty of fiber, such as organically-grown fresh produce. Check out: "Environmental Working Group's Clean 15 List", which are relatively free of pesticides. As far as pesticides go, they are said to be okay to eat as an alternative to organic versions. Foods high in fiber are also rich in prebiotics, which feed the beneficial bacteria. Some

foods high in prebiotic fibers include asparagus, fresh onions, and fresh garlic.

2. Eat plenty of foods rich in Vitamin C. Vitamin C helps the body produce glutathione, a liver compound that decreases toxins in the body.

3. Water is essential to overall health for countless reasons and is the absolute best beverage for our bodies. Shoot for about two quarts (four pints) of high-quality water each day (unless you have a condition where you have to limit fluid intake). I use spring and heavily filtered/purified water (without chlorine as it can kill the beneficial bacteria in the gut). High-quality water flushes out toxins. If your urine is pale, then you are most likely drinking enough water for your body. Also, drinking a glass every couple hours will make you feel more alert. Be careful not to gulp liquids though, as that can put too much strain the kidneys, so drink slowly!

4. Take a salt bath: This type of therapeutic bath will help you sweat out toxins and also contains magnesium to relax your muscles. At first, try this at nighttime before bed, as the initial one might make you feel a bit like a zombie (while you are sleeping this feeling will be just fine). Use rock salt (such as 100% Pure Himalayan) or Epsom salt. Himalayan salt domes are also available, which help with detoxification and more! As a side note, Epsom salt baths can be quite beneficial for arthritis sufferers.

5. Use onions to draw out toxins! Place thick slices of organic onions (room temperature) on a plate and then sit outside when it is hot (or in a sauna) with your feet sitting on the slices. Then imagine the onions drawing out all the toxins in your body! The natural healing powers will go to work through your skin (trans-dermal application), helping to

purify your blood, decreasing bacteria and other unwanted microbes, as well as absorbing toxins.

6. Sweat in a sauna (if tolerated) so your body can eliminate wastes through perspiration. Saunas are a great way to detoxify your body! The infrared type, in particular, can be highly effective. See if there are any near you. They are even available for sale to have in your home.

7. Regular exercise is one of the best ways to detoxify: Activities such as brisk walking, jumping-rope, and dancing are excellent. Be sure to work up a sweat! Exercise accelerates toxin removal through our largest organ of elimination, the skin when we sweat. Both breathing and sweating are great ways to release toxins from the body. Mild to moderate exercise is best, as intense exercise for long periods of time can actually increase inflammation. Shoot for at least thirty minutes five times per week (as tolerated and if possible). Also try qigong, which includes movements and breathing that target detoxification and cleansing, as well as many other exercises that have specific health benefits.

"Sweat is just the body wringing out toxins, negativity and bad energy."

~ Emily Barrett "Spry Living"

- Also see the "Exercise" chapter for more information.

Help Detoxify Your Body with the Following Superfoods:

• If allergic or intolerant to any of the following, or a healthcare provider or research states that you cannot eat a certain food due to a particular condition or medication, or the "The Blood Type Diet®" plan states you should avoid a certain food, then feel free to move on to the next superfood.

Remember: Organic is best!

Carrots and Beets: These vegetables are superfoods with countless health benefits. Carrots are high in glutathione, a protein that assists with liver detoxification. Carrots and beets also contain plant-flavonoids and beta-carotene. Eating carrots and beats helps stimulate and improve overall liver function. Steamed beets (already prepared) can be found in most grocery store produce sections. So, not only are they healthy to eat, they are fast and quite tasty too!

Asparagus: An excellent diuretic, asparagus helps in the cleansing process and assists the liver and kidneys.

Spinach: Raw spinach is a major source of glutathione that triggers the "toxin cleansing" enzymes of the liver. On a side note, it is easy to store in the refrigerator for relatively long periods of time compared to other types of "lettuce".

Leafy Green Vegetables: These vegetables are extremely high in plant chlorophylls which absorb all sorts of environmental toxins from the bloodstream. They also increase bile production (the substance which removes waste from organs and blood), as well as neutralize heavy metals, chemicals, and pesticides. This all lowers the burden on the liver. Leafy green vegetables can be eaten raw, cooked (but do not overcook), juiced (although beneficial fiber is then removed), or included in smoothies (a high-quality blender will be needed).

Cruciferous Vegetables: Vegetables such as broccoli, cauliflower, cabbage, garden cress, bok choy, Brussels sprouts, and similar green-leaf vegetables are high in Vitamin C and soluble fiber, and contain multiple nutrients and phytochemicals as well. Cruciferous vegetables contain glucosinolates which are under research for potential healing properties and may reduce the risk of some types of cancer. Eating vegetables such as broccoli and cauliflower will likely increase glucosinolates in your system. This adds to enzyme production in the liver that helps flush out and neutralize toxins, including chemicals, pesticides, pharmaceuticals, and carcinogens. Cabbage, like broccoli and cauliflower, can help stimulate activation of two crucial liver detoxification enzymes that flush out toxins. Brussels sprouts are high in sulfur and antioxidant glucosinolate which force the liver to release enzymes that block damage from environmental and dietary toxins.

Tomatoes: Tomatoes have abundant amounts of glutathione (liver detoxifier). They also contain lycopene which is known for several health benefits (please note, though, that some people need to avoid tomatoes).

Avocados: Avocados help the body produce glutathione, and are also nutrient-dense. The healthy fats in avocados are also essential during the body's natural detoxification process. They promote the release of bile from the gallbladder, allowing for the elimination of toxins and the absorption of fat-soluble vitamins including Vitamin A, D, E, and K. Avocados also contain Vitamin E, folate, Vitamin B5, and potassium.

Onions: Experts like Dr. Jonathan Stegall, an integrative medicine provider, have highlighted the beneficial health properties of onions: "Onions contain a high amount of sulfur compounds, which not only give onions their recognizable smell, but are also powerful detoxifying agents." With more than one hundred sulfur compounds (which are what cause the eyes to tear), onions can also help prevent and treat ailments, such as diabetes and heart disease. In addition, they exhibit antimicrobial activity (including antiviral).

Citrus Fruits: Limes and lemons contain high amounts of Vitamin C, which helps stimulate the liver and aids the synthesizing of toxic materials into substances that can be absorbed by water. Drinking freshly squeezed lime or lemon juice in the morning helps stimulate the liver. Oranges can assist in digestion and help to cleanse the body. Not only can eating oranges help to clean out the digestive system, it also fights unwanted microbes, which can improve overall immunity. Grapefruit is another source of the "liver cleansing" glutathione. It is also high in Vitamin C and antioxidants, which can boost the production of the liver detoxification enzymes and increase the natural cleansing process of the liver. Vitamin C also helps the body absorb more iron. So consider increasing your citrus fruits (as tolerated of course).

Wild Blueberries: The "wild" types of blueberries are particularly good for detoxification, especially from heavy metals, according to Anthony William, Medical Medium. You can most likely find them in your local supermarket freezer. I love eating them right out of the bag. It reminds me of candy or ice cream!

Apples: Apples are high in pectin and other substances that can cleanse and release toxins from the digestive tract. They can also make it easier for the liver to handle the toxic load during the cleansing process. Eating fruits on an empty stomach may also give them more detoxifying power.

Turmeric: This is a great spice for liver health and helps boost liver detoxification by assisting enzymes that actively flush out dietary carcinogens. There is also evidence that confirms turmeric is an anti-inflammatory, possibly more effective than ibuprofen. There seem to be countless health benefits from turmeric! In addition to cooking with it, it is available as a supplement. Another term used for turmeric, in pill form, is curcumin or curcuma longa. Adding black pepper and a bit of fat are ways to help increase turmeric absorption. Turmeric assists many people, but it is not for everyone, especially in high amounts. Please do your research and also see the "Natural Supplements" chapter about Th1 and Th2 dominance issues.

Garlic: Loaded with sulfur that activates liver enzymes, garlic helps the body flush out toxins. It also has high amounts of allicin and selenium, which aid in liver cleansing. Raw garlic is especially powerful. If raw garlic creates GI discomfort, consuming it on a full stomach can help decrease any irritation. Also, fresh parsley can help to mitigate garlic odor.

Cilantro and Parsley: These herbs are known for their detoxification abilities, especially with heavy metals. A word of caution: because they can easily absorb heavy metals, anytime during the growing process this can occur.

Do not grow them in soil that might be contaminated with metals. If the herb has a metallic taste it may be contaminated. You can buy bunches of organic cilantro at many local markets, and it will keep nicely in the refrigerator. It is nutritious and has many healing benefits. I like cilantro on almost anything that is not sweet, and always enjoy it with my Mexican-style dishes. A favorite herb among chefs, parsley is aromatic and also commonly used in herbal medicines. As a natural diuretic, parsley can help reduce toxins in the urinary tract. Fresh parsley can also be used to deodorize the mouth. Parsley and cilantro are quite easy to grow and thus have on-hand anytime!

Green Tea: Full of plant antioxidants known as catechins, green tea assists with liver function. Green tea benefits many people, but it is not for everyone, especially in high amounts. Please do your research and also see the "Natural Supplements" chapter about Th1 and Th2 dominance issues.

Dandelion Root: Dandelion root assists the liver in breaking down fats and producing amino acids. It is also used for liver cleanses. It can be eaten, as well as used as a beverage. In addition, I have seen "liver detoxification and support" supplements that contain it.

Cold-Pressed Organic Oils: Oils such as olive and flaxseed can be major supports for the liver, providing the body with liquid bases that absorb toxins.

Fermented Foods: Foods such as are sauerkraut, natural pickles, kimchi, olives, beet kvass, and other fermented vegetables can help your body rid itself of toxins such as heavy metals and pesticides. Most health experts agree that fermented foods are beneficial for health (but it is important to note that some think one should be cautious of fermented foods).

Walnuts: These nuts are an excellent source of glutathione, Omega-3 fatty acids (in the raw version), and the amino acid arginine. These all support the normal liver cleansing actions, especially in detoxifying ammonia. Eating a few walnuts a day may also help reduce the risk of Alzheimer's and slow the progression of the disease. A 2014 study from the New York State Institute for Basic Research in Developmental Disabilities found that adding walnuts to the diets of mice (with the mouse version of Alzheimer's) boosted learning skills and memory, reduced anxiety, and improved motor development. The amount of walnuts added to the mouse diet was the equivalent to a human portion (one ounce to one and a half ounces a day). The researchers performed this study following findings that walnut extracts showed activity against the oxidative damage caused by amyloid protein (the major component of amyloid plaques characteristic of Alzheimer's disease). The high antioxidant content of walnuts may have helped protect the mouse brain from the degeneration seen in Alzheimer's. The study also suggested that adding walnuts delayed the onset or prevented Alzheimer's in the mice. As a side note, always make sure to chew nuts well (until they are liquefied in your mouth) before swallowing. I order my high-quality nuts (and other healthy snacks) from Nuts.com.

Flaxseeds: Full of vitamins, minerals, Omega-3 fatty acids, and fiber, flaxseeds support intestinal health. They can absorb toxic compounds from food, "clean" the intestines, and supply the body with lecithin, which stimulates the metabolism of fat. Flaxseeds help eliminate toxins from the body, normalize metabolism, as well as tamp down blood sugar and appetite.

Algae: Algaes, such as spirulina and chlorella, can be used to help with heavy metal detoxification. They are effective at binding toxins and eliminating them from the body, meanwhile actually reducing some of the side effects associated with detoxification. Spirulina and chlorella also have been shown to exhibit strong healing and regenerating capabilities in many people. They are filled with beneficial nutrients which work together in a synergistic way to provide energy and vitality. It is important to find a processer of spirulina or chlorella that takes steps to ensure a clean and digestible product, also free of additives. Doing some research can reveal which brands are the most reputable. I often see algae, such as chlorella, used along with cilantro as they seem to work quite well together in detoxifying the body from heavy metals. Note that some people should avoid chlorella, especially in high amounts. See the "Natural Supplements" chapter which contains information on Th1/Th2 dominance issues.

Switch to Alternative Grains: Gluten-rich grains, such as wheat, tend to increase the load on the liver's detoxification function and enzyme production. Consider alternatives like rice, tapioca, buckwheat, quinoa, and flaxseeds. Also, flours from foods such as lentils as well as almonds can provide a base in recipes, replacing grain flour. It is important to note that many people have reported tremendous positive results after going completely grain-free.

Radishes, Artichokes, and Horseradish: Radishes and artichokes can be excellent detoxifying foods. Studies are also suggesting that horseradish is linked to the activation of certain detoxifying enzymes and has cancer-fighting properties.

Milk thistle is an herbal supplement which has been known to cleanse, protect, and support the liver. Milk thistle is actually clinically proven to repair liver damage. It is a strong antioxidant bioflavonoid. Talk with your healthcare provider and do your research if you are interested in trying an herbal supplement (also check out the "Natural Supplements" chapter of this book).

Increasing your magnesium levels can further assist in your body's detoxification process.

Again, I have personally found the following nutritional smoothie mix to be extremely helpful for detoxification, restoring gut health, and reducing inflammation: MediClear Plus® by Thorne Research® (available online). This supplemental smoothie mix is not to be used ongoing (short-term basis only). There has also been a recommended diet plan associated with the smoothie mix that many have found helpful in aiding in the achievement of the above goals.

Detoxifying heavy metals (especially aluminum) with silica:

Silica has recently been found to have multiple vital nutritional benefits, and in addition PubMed has acknowledged it as an antidote for aluminum poisoning and a detoxification agent for heavy metals. Both aluminum toxicity and brain tissue calcification are linked to Alzheimer's disease (a form of dementia). Now it has been discovered that silica can be supplemented to help prevent dementia as well. It can also be used as an adjunct with other Alzheimer's "treatments", such as pure cold pressed coconut oil.

Aluminum, which has been referred to as a neurotoxin, apparently accumulates over time in tissue that does not have a rapid cellular turnover. The slow turnover tissues are contained in bones, as well as heart and brain areas. The brain and nervous system are where diseases such as Alzheimer's, Parkinson's, MS, chronic fatigue, and other neurological and autoimmune diseases manifest (including conditions such as autism).

Unfortunately, there is no lack of aluminum in our daily lives. It is in beverage and food containers, foil, cookware, cigarette smoke, some personal care products, vaccines, and more. Dr. Chris Exley, PhD, has spent almost two decades researching the effects of aluminum on the body. He refers to the period of time from the early 20th Century until now as the "Age of Aluminum". Interestingly, Dr. Exley claims that the current mining aluminum and using it in so many ways corresponds to the marked increase in specific types of diseases and health conditions.

Dr. Exley has recommended a few types of mineral waters that are high in silica. A current favorite seems to be FIJI® (I have found it in almost all supermarkets). He claimed positive results occurred with "vaccine injured" children drinking water high in silica, but that there are other good, less expensive, sources as well.

Horsetail is an inexpensive herbal source of silica. It has been around for centuries, and mostly forgotten until recent research discovered more attributes. Until then, it was used mostly as a diuretic or kidney stone treatment. Horsetail tea is an option (I have read it must be boiled in order to increase effectiveness). It seems that horsetail is not recommended for long-term use. Therefore it is best to use short-term just to address a presenting concern.

Foods that can help keep your silica levels higher include: unrefined whole grains, alfalfa sprouts, nuts, seeds, celery, peppers, carrots, potatoes, beets, onions, tomatoes, and cucumbers. Silica is also found in hemp as well as nettle leaves. There are other substances which contain silica that you may want to consider as well.

Of course, I need to emphasize that you will need to conduct current research and work with your healthcare provider prior to and during any detoxification protocol.

- Also see the "Natural Supplements" chapter for more on detoxification.

Chapter Forty-Seven

Anti-inflammatory Foods

The running thread linking a wide variety of increasingly common health problems (autoimmune diseases, obesity, diabetes, cancer, heart disease, and even mental health concerns) is chronic inflammation. Chronic inflammation releases powerful unwanted oxidants. When a person is at the point of actually having an autoimmune disease, the body is then at the extreme of inflammation, where the body can seem as if it is attacking itself. Therefore autoimmune diseases can be seen as extreme inflammation. While reducing the effects of stress and getting regular exercise are key components to decreasing inflammation in the body, we can also add certain anti-inflammatory foods to our diets, all the while beginning to eliminate refined sugar, highly processed food, and artificial ingredients, to optimize health.

"Today, it is widely accepted among doctors and scientists that

inflammation is the root cause of a whole host of chronic diseases,

including heart disease, diabetes and cancer. And, when your body is in a

constant state of inflammation, it not only can cause you to get sick, but it

also speeds up the aging process – a term known as inflamm-aging."

~ Dr. Christiane Northrup

The following foods are anti-inflammatory super heroes. **Eat them as often as possible:**

- If allergic or intolerant to any of the following, or a healthcare provider or research states that you cannot eat a certain food due to a particular condition or medication, or the "The Blood Type Diet®" plan states you should avoid a certain food, then feel free to move on to the next superfood.

Remember: Organic is best!

<u>Fish and Omega-3:</u>   Fish such as salmon, mackerel (Atlantic), anchovies, trout, herring, and sardines are all high in the extremely beneficial Omega-3 anti-inflammatory fats. When it comes to fat, this is one type you do not want to avoid. Two key ones (EPA and DHA) are mainly found in fish. Look for "wild" as that is usually best. While eating more fatty fish can be quite beneficial, certain types are likely to have higher levels of mercury, PCBs, and other toxins. I urge you to do current research and limit those types of fish in

your diet. High-quality eggs can also be a source of Omega-3. ALA (alpha-linolenic acid), another Omega-3 fatty acid, comes to us from plant sources such as seeds and nuts. Your body needs Omega-3 essential fatty acids to function and they deliver large health benefits as well.

Vegetables: Most North Americans are not getting enough vegetation in their diets. Shoot for as many servings as possible per day. Make them vibrant and colorful. For most people, I suggest eating at least some raw vegetation daily (wash them well, prior to enjoying). If you are not used to eating all that fiber, try starting low and working your way up to more. Broccoli, spinach, kale, collard greens, and rainbow chard are full of Vitamin E, which protects the body from pro-inflammatory cytokines. Eating kale can decrease iron deficiency, which is another bonus. Dark green and cruciferous vegetables have high concentrations of minerals and phytochemicals. Cauliflower can be a satisfying replacement for grains or starchy foods, and has countless healing benefits. Green leafy vegetables contain magnesium, which is helpful for blood pressure, and they are low-glycemic, which means they will not cause insulin spikes. Bell peppers contain capsaicin, which assists in reducing pain and inflammation. Tomatoes are high in lycopene, which is well known for helping to reduce inflammation in the body (for those who are not sensitive to nightshades). Cooking the tomatoes will increase the lycopene and total antioxidant content, according to the Journal of Agricultural and Food Chemistry. Also according to the same journal, consuming red beets regularly can protect against "certain oxidative stress-related disorders in humans". It is not a secret that celery is another superfood! Eating just one stick of celery a day can make a difference in your health. It contains a high amount of anti-inflammatory compounds, it is an excellent diuretic, it helps remove uric acid crystals from around painful joints, and assists in lowering blood pressure.

Further increase your vegetable intake by trying "noodles" made with zucchini using a special slicer (and can be bought pre-made). Add raw veggies to smoothies in order to increase your body's ability to absorb the high amount of vital nutrients, as well as give your digestive system a bit of a break, all so it can heal faster. As a side note, there are mixers out there that can handle foods like raw carrots, great for smoothies.

Avocados: In addition to all the nutrients, highly beneficial fats, and fiber, avocados help to tamp down inflammation in the body as well as the brain. They also can assist in lowering bad cholesterol and regulating blood sugar. Countless recipes can be made from avocados as the base, including desserts! My spiritual counselor had a good idea for storing avocados and keeping them in prime condition. She buys them from a reputable market while they are still rock-hard. She then keeps them refrigerated until about one or two days before she wants to use them. After being out of the refrigerator for approximately one to two days, they are ready to use! Of course they will not store in the refrigerator forever, but they will keep nicely and for much longer than if not refrigerated. I have just started to do this and it works beautifully! Packaged avocado can also be store-bought to have on-hand for the times a fresh avocado is not available. Use as a dip, spread, or side to a meal or snack.

Sweet Potatoes: Nutrient dense sweet potatoes are another superfood that can help decrease inflammation. They are also known to satisfy a sweet tooth. Many delicious and healthy dessert foods are made with them. Look for deep orange color when choosing your sweet potatoes. Store them at cool room temperature in a breathable bag or container. Enjoy promptly.

Fruits and Berries: Blueberries, cherries (as well as a bit of watered-down unsweetened cherry juice), pineapple, raspberries, strawberries, cranberries, apricots, and apples are examples of fruits that can help reduce inflammation in the body. Berries are high in anthocyanins, which are powerful antioxidants that are known to be anti-inflammatory. Anthocyanin pigments and associated flavonoids have demonstrated ability to protect against a myriad of diseases. It is important to note that blueberries in particular can protect against intestinal inflammation. Blueberries contain antioxidants which work to neutralize free radicals that are linked to the development of conditions such as cancer and cardiovascular disease. They are high in Vitamin C and can also improve heart and brain health, reduce cancer risk, and fight urinary tract infections. Wild blueberries are especially powerful for both detoxification and inflammation reduction, and can be found in the freezer section of most markets. Fresh pineapples contain a substance known as bromelain which is an enzyme that has anti-inflammatory characteristics. Pineapple helps combat infections and bacteria, and the juice has actually been found to be more effective at helping to stop coughing than traditional cough syrup. The CDC has stated that only around fifteen percent of adults in the United States are eating the recommended amount of fruit, and that percentage is even lower for vegetable guidelines. Hopefully the number will increase as more people are educated on the power of fruits and vegetables. As a side note: always make sure fresh fruits and vegetables are cleaned well before enjoying.

"Fruit often gets a bad rap these days. It's lumped into the same basket as refined sugars like cane sugar, sucrose, high fructose corn syrup, and agave. But fruit is nothing like these other sugars, and the current

misinformation around fruit and the resulting fruit fear is having serious

consequences on our health and survival. Fruit is simply the innocent

casualty of the war on sugar. In truth, fruit is vital to our livelihood.

Limiting fruit in your diet will increase your chances of illness and shorten

your expected lifespan. With the challenges we face in today's world, we

need more fruit in our diets than ever before."

~ **Anthony William, Medical Medium**

Nuts and Seeds: Raw walnuts, raw pecans, sesame seeds, chia seeds, and flaxseeds all contain Omega-3 fats that reduce inflammation. According to recent research, consuming a handful of walnuts daily can help keep you safe from cardiovascular ailments. Researchers have also revealed that it betters the cholesterol levels and elasticity of blood vessels which will improve circulation (within four hours after consuming the nuts or nut oil). Dr. Penny Kris Eterton, professor of nutrition at Penn State University in Pennsylvania, said: "By consuming a handful of walnuts or walnut oil for at least four days in a week, you will greatly decrease the risk of heart ailments". Walnut oil is extremely helpful for the wholeness of the endothelial cells which have a vital role in the body because they line the blood vessels. My absolute favorite place to order nuts and seeds is from Nuts.com. Please note that a few types of nuts should probably not be eaten raw, especially in high amounts. Please do current research before beginning to include raw nuts in your diet, and always buy from a trusted source.

Turmeric, and other Herbs and Spices: Turmeric, black pepper, ginger, saffron, Ceylon cinnamon, garlic, basil, rosemary, sage, thyme, and oregano contain nutrients and help fight inflammation in many people. Turmeric is a known anti-inflammatory and so much more! Turmeric is one of the most potent spices and is associated with numerous health benefits. Not only is it one of the most impressive free radical scavengers, it has also been shown to support brain health, protect cell integrity, and even help in mood stabilization. New research is showing that turmeric may also play a key role in thyroid support. Mix it with black pepper and some fat for better absorption. (Again, turmeric is not for everyone, especially in high amounts. Do your research and also see the "Natural Supplements" chapter for more on Th1 and Th2 dominance issues). Ginger contains the anti-inflammatory compound gingerol, which provides free radical protection. Raw garlic has numerous health benefits. It is best to consume raw garlic at the end of a meal if you are concerned about any digestive upset. Fresh parsley after the garlic can help to dissipate the odor. I like using fresh herbs as well as freeze-dried. Remember that healthy herbs and spices are great to use in place of salt and sweeteners. As a side note, to ensure freshness, be sure to watch the expiration dates on all of your herbs and spices. It is important to replace them frequently. Store them in a cool dry place, away from direct sunlight.

Dark Chocolate: Once in a while a bit of high-quality dark chocolate can be a good thing to eat. I am talking about chocolate that is at least 70% pure cocoa, not highly processed, and no more than about one ounce at a time. The cocoa solids contain healthy compounds called flavonols, which have anti-inflammatory and antioxidant properties. There are growing numbers of recently discovered health benefits of dark chocolate. Try breaking bars up into pieces and keeping them in a baggie for a bit of a chocolate treat. You can also add unsweetened 70% pure cocoa to smoothies, and include some Stevia In The Raw® for sweetener. High quality cacao nibs can be another option.

Green Tea: Like a liquid vegetable, green tea has anti-inflammatory benefits. Start with a small cup and increase as tolerated. Please note that, although there are proven health benefits, green tea is not for everybody. Please do your research and also see the "Natural Supplements" chapter on Th1 and Th2 dominance issues. Also, remember that green tea has some caffeine, therefore if you have any caffeine-related issues (or if you are not able to have caffeine due to a certain condition), then green tea is not for you.

Chamomile Tea: A naturally occurring substance in chamomile provides potent anti-inflammatory and blood thinning abilities. (See also the "Chamomile" chapter).

Onions: Onions contain several anti-inflammatory compounds that contribute to reducing symptoms that are associated with a host of inflammatory conditions such as RA (studies have actually linked onions with arthritis relief), the allergic inflammatory response of asthma, and respiratory congestion that occurs with colds. Onions contain compounds that inhibit enzymes that generate inflammation. Vitamin C and quercetin work together contributing to this beneficial effect. Quercetin is a plant pigment (flavonoid) found in onions. Onions are a great choice during cold and flu season!

Fermented Foods: Foods such as sauerkraut, natural pickles, miso, kimchee, olives, beet kvass, and others, can help naturally "reseed" your gut with beneficial bacteria. High quality yogurt (be careful of the sugar content) and kefir are also options, if you eat dairy products. Fermented foods, like cultured vegetables, can supply your body with beneficial bacteria that aid in digestion and provide detoxification support. Made from fermented cabbage, sauerkraut is not only rich in healthy live cultures and vitamins, but it also can help reduce allergy symptoms in many people. Kimchi is a probiotic fermented food you can consider adding to your diet, assuming you can handle the spice. Optimizing gut flora is important for a well-functioning immune system, and helps ward off chronic inflammation. The majority of inflammatory diseases seem to start in the gut, at least partly due to an imbalanced microbiome. Tofu and tempeh, the traditionally eaten forms of fermented soy, provide protein and other nutrients. They also can be anti-inflammatory. Fermentation adds extra nutrients and probiotics ("good" bacteria) to soy. Again, most health care experts (but not all) would agree that fermented foods are beneficial for health.

Coconut: Natural coconut products have excellent therapeutic benefits for many people. They are anti-inflammatory, antimicrobial (help to decrease bacteria, fungi, parasites, and viruses). Coconut products can of course be eaten, but the oil can also be used on skin and hair. In addition, it is currently considered one of the healthiest oils for cooking. Regardless of type of cooking oil used however, from what I have learned moderation seems to be key.

In order to reduce inflammation, here are some foods and substances I suggest avoiding:

- Anything artificial (especially artificial food dyes- they are linked to severe behavioral problems in children).
- Margarine and other trans fats (artificially processed fats/partially hydrogenated oils).

- Deep fried foods and commercially baked goods (most are fried in trans-fat or contain trans-fat).

- Sugar (especially refined or processed sugars).

- Highly processed soy (especially non-organic).

- Mono-Sodium Glutamate (MSG).

- Any food or substance that you are allergic to, or cannot tolerate well or digest.

- Excessive amounts of alcohol.

- Excess consumption of corn or corn products (especially non-organic).

- Too much Omega-6 and not enough Omega-3.

- High amounts of flour from grains.

- Excess consumption of caffeine.

- Gluten and dairy products (especially non-organic) (these can contribute to inflammation in many people).

There is emerging evidence suggesting that consuming too many animal products (such as meat) is linked to disease. Therefore, I suggest getting the majority of your nutrients from plant sources. I mean, has the idea of "Eat more vegetables" ever really been controversial?

Also, I suggest limiting foods that have been cooked at extremely high temperatures, especially if cooked with vegetable oil (such as soybean or corn oils). Current research states that a few of the healthiest oils to cook with are coconut and olive (just watch the temperature levels with your oils, and moderation is still in order).

Chapter Forty-Eight

Make Sure You Include the Following in Your Diet

The following help decrease nerve sensitivities and swelling, improve cognition, and keep the immune system healthy (also see the "Natural Supplements" chapter for more information):

Omega-3: Again, there are countless benefits to ingesting Omega-3 essential fatty acids. Directly affecting cellular function, this fatty acid found in fish (and a few other foods such as raw nuts, seeds, and certain types of eggs) can help improve cognition, minimize nerve sensitivity, and help balance the immune system.

B-Complex: B vitamins directly influence the nervous system's proper functioning, and fight against nerve issues (such as tingling and tenderness). Some food sources include: chicken, fish, legumes, nuts, and eggs.

Magnesium: This mineral is necessary for muscle flexibility as well as bone, protein, and fatty acid formation. It is also needed in order to make new cells, relax muscles, clot blood, activate B vitamins, and aid in calcium absorption (helps prevent osteoporosis). It assists with irritability, restlessness, sleep, blood pressure, pregnancy and lactation issues, migraines, and serotonin production as well. Getting enough magnesium is an ideal remedy for stress as it naturally calms the nervous system. It also supports detoxification systems in the body. Some food sources of magnesium include: dark green vegetables, avocados, nuts, seeds, legumes, whole grain oats, brown rice, quinoa, fish, meat, bananas, high-quality dark chocolate (at least 70% cocoa), coconut water, seaweed, and blackstrap molasses. Consume more magnesium-rich foods to help reduce symptoms of magnesium deficiency. You may be surprised how much better it can make you feel!

Vitamin C: This nutrient helps fight stress, supports the immune system, and helps reduce swelling. Food sources include fresh fruits and vegetables (such as berries, grapes, citrus fruits, tomatoes, and green vegetables).

Water: High-quality water increases oxygen and nutrient circulation throughout the body, and helps eliminate waste.

Foods for relaxation: Foods that contain calcium, magnesium, and Vitamin B6 are known to have tranquilizing effects. Green leafy vegetables, nuts, apricots, and bananas are just a few that have the ability to help you feel calmer. Meat, eggs, and pumpkin seeds are examples of foods which contain tryptophan, an essential amino acid that turns into serotonin, which enhances mood and regulates sleep.

If you have joint pain, make sure you are getting enough of the following vitamins: Vitamin A, C, D, and E.

Arthritis and low boron? Worldwide evidence is now starting to link low intake of boron with increased levels of arthritis, which could add to the proof that arthritis is not simply just part of the aging process, as Western medicine may have us believe. With so many people suffering, it is time to start considering this mineral (along with other nutrients, lifestyle changes, and alternative interventions), instead of just jumping to symptom-suppressing synthetic medications. Some foods that contain boron include: raisins, dried apricots, prunes, dates, avocados, peanut butter, walnuts, brazil nuts, broccoli, pears, peaches, kiwis, honey, chick peas, legumes, carrots, beets, celery, olives, red grapes, red apples, and oranges. Additional supplementation may also be necessary.

A health care professional might also be able to guide you as to which foods to incorporate into your diet in order to help heal your particular condition(s). For example, my former acupuncturist (who also practices Chinese medicine) provided a list of foods to add or increase in my diet in order to assist in my particular healing process. Your health care professional might also be able to recommend which foods to avoid for your particular condition(s).

Iodine: Research has shown that a lack of iodine may lead to enlargement of the thyroid gland, fatigue, slow metabolism, weight gain, autism, weakness of the immune system, and possibly even mood disorders such as anxiety and depression. The good news is that there are many popular foods that contain naturally occurring iodine, all of which are easy to incorporate into your diet.

The following are some natural foods which contain iodine:

- Navy Beans

- Strawberries

- Cranberries

- Potatoes (with peel)

- Bananas

- Eggs

- Seafood

- Sea Vegetables

- Himalayan pink salt (make sure it comes from a quality source)

National Nutrient Database:

It is important to note that there is a highly useful comprehensive database of countless foods that can be searched and sorted according to specific nutrients. This database is called National Nutrient Database and the website is: ndb.nal.usda.gov.

- If you truly feel that you are absolutely unable to dramatically change your diet at this time, according to Anne Procyk, Naturopathic Physician, consider two easy changes that can have a dramatic effect on your health: adding more vegetables and including protein with every meal.

Eating a well-balanced diet with plenty of fresh vegetables and fruits can help you feel much more alert and full of vitality. Having beautiful healthy foods around (like a well-stocked lovely bowl of fresh fruit) will help you avoid the junk! There are some cookbooks available that aid in incorporating more vegetables into the diet if it is difficult (due to preference to not eat plain vegetables, or having small children to cook for at home). According to Anne Procyk, Naturopathic Physician, you can try using cookbooks such as "Deceptively Delicious" by Jessica Seinfeld. In addition, Dr. Procyk stated that modeling behaviors can also do the trick if you are trying to get someone else to eat more vegetables.

Now you have a more clear idea of which items you can include on your list! Also when you add them, as well as when you prepare meals (and perhaps bring along with you on outings), you can tell yourself it is one of the significant ways you are self-nurturing!

Chapter Forty-Nine

Chamomile

The chamomile plant is pretty miraculous! There seems to be countless reasons to drink chamomile tea, in addition to the more obvious relaxation effect. Chamomile has been used for centuries for anxiety, depression, insomnia, pain relief, and even as a natural anti-fungal (it can help eliminate yeast such as Candida). Amazingly, the essential oil of chamomile has been shown to kill breast cancer cells, by triggering programmed cell death. Researchers are discovering that chamomile also helps fight several other cancers including prostate, lung, leukemia, and more. It contains a high amount of the anticancer flavonoid called apigenin, which is otherwise difficult to receive in diet alone (parsley, oregano, and celery are food sources). One cup of chamomile tea contains about 2 mg of apigenin, which is four times the daily intake of most American adults! The amount can also make a difference in cancer risk. In addition, research is now confirming it improves sleep and may relieve depression. Quite incredibly, it has also been found to decrease insulin levels, insulin resistance, LDL cholesterol, as well as triglycerides in adults with type II diabetes.

Chamomile, often used for teas, is alkalizing with anti-inflammatory effects. It also has a calming effect on the nervous system and exerts antibacterial effects against several pathogen bacteria, including E. coli, streptococcus, and staphylococcus. All according to herbalist Brigitte Mars, author of the book "Healing Herbal Teas".

I currently enjoy chamomile tea on a daily basis, as it is a nice sweet-tasting herb. It is a good idea to let the tea steep as long as possible before drinking, in order to get the most benefit into your cup.

Roman Chamomile therapeutic essential oil can be extremely relaxing and help induce sleep. It has been used for hundreds of years as an herbal medicine. Aromatically, roman chamomile supports restful sleep, while topically it can reduce mental stress and associated aches and pains. It is also used for inflamed skin, arthritis, PMS, and hormonal balance. At the time of this writing, ADK Aromatherapy "Etsy's Premiere Aromatherapy & Essential Oils Shoppe" is one place that carries chamomile essential oils.

There are some possible side-effects to chamomile and some people should avoid it. Please research trusted sources (and review with your healthcare provider) before beginning a regime of chamomile. As always, start with a small amount and work your way up to more, as tolerated. Use with some caution and follow all directions.

Chapter Fifty

Coconut

C oconut oil seems to have a million uses, and that also includes its therapeutic abilities. Coconut products in general can be a healthy (and therapeutic) diet addition for many people. There are numerous high-quality brands available.

Some say that if you are going to ingest the oil without cooking first, it should be the "refined" version in order to insure purity. Oil you use for cooking can be "unrefined" because cooking would eliminate any impurities. That said, I have never heard of anyone getting ill from eating unrefined coconut oil. One reason is probably due to the fact that the oil itself is antimicrobial (including antiviral). When using for skin or hair cream, it is fine to use the unrefined type. My massage therapist uses coconut oil frequently with clients. The natural aroma is heavenly!

At the time of this writing, coconut oil has been noted by multiple sources as one of the healthiest oils to use for cooking. It can withstand a high amount of heat. You can also use it as a spread just like butter. However, in regards to the use of oil that is not considered an Omega-3, moderation is important.

I would also like to add that next time you have a craving for a sweet treat, you can try a bit of delicious coconut water and see how it satisfies and in a healthy way!

Chapter Fifty-One

Bone Broth

My spiritual counselor recommended incorporating bone broth into my diet due to its countless therapeutic benefits. Interestingly, bone broth is often used to treat children with autism and other disorders thought to be rooted in gut dysfunction. But, just about anyone with allergies, autoimmune issues, or less than optimal gut health can benefit from it, as it is designed to heal leaky gut.

Again, if your gut is permeable, partially undigested food, toxins, viruses, yeast, and bacteria may pass through your intestines and access your bloodstream. This is known as leaky gut. When your intestinal lining is repeatedly damaged, the cells can then become unable to do their job properly, like impairment in processing and utilizing nutrients and enzymes that are vital to digestion. Eventually, digestion and absorption of nutrients are affected. As time goes on, your body then initiates an attack on the "foreign invaders". It responds with inflammation, allergic reactions, and other symptoms related to a variety of diseases.

Leaky gut is thought to be the root of many allergies as well as autoimmune disorders. Again, some say that all individuals with autoimmune disease have leaky gut. When combined with toxic overload, you then have issues that can lead to neurological-related disorders like autism and ADHD.

To get the most benefit from bone broth, and its intestinal healing properties, it is best to avoid inflammatory foods and substances while incorporating bone broth into your diet. Also remove foods that are difficult to digest, anything you are intolerant of, and foods you know you are allergic to. Again, I highly recommend following the "The Blood Type Diet®" as much as you possibly can as well.

Bone broth is easily digested by most people. It also provides profound immune system optimizing components that are foundational building blocks and is almost always included in effective treatment plans for autoimmune conditions. Adding vegetables like carrots and celery while cooking your bone broth gives additional "easy-to-digest" healing nutrients.

As your gut begins to be restored and your health improves, some foods might be able to be added back in. Bone broth can still remain a staple because it is so nourishing. Even if you do not think you have gut issues, it can still be beneficial to include in your diet, especially during cold and flu season.

There are numerous bone broth recipes online, and cookbooks are also readily available. Homemade is best, but if you cannot currently make you own, you may purchase it. There are online options for pre-made organic bone broth, and some supermarkets carry it as well. Located in the freezer at my local Fruitful Yield health food store is the high-quality Bonafide™ brand that I enjoy. It is said that the best and most effective bone broth has a gel-like consistency when refrigerated, and the one I purchase definitely qualifies.

- Also see the "Leaky Gut" chapter for more information.

Chapter Fifty-Two

Dietician Services

Your journey back to health may also include a registered dietician or a nutritionist. I recommend seeing one who specializes in your general condition, as he or she will likely have information more specific to you and your situation. My preference would be one who is holistic, alternative, or natural health-minded as well.

In my opinion, dieticians and nutritionists might not be able to tell you with 100% accuracy what you should eat, because I believe everyone is a bit different and you will have to listen to your own body. Your specific food preferences should not be completely overlooked either and need to be discussed as well. However, they can guide you, answer questions, make sure you are getting enough nutrition, offer healthier suggestions (for example, using fresh avocado instead of mayonnaise), link you up with certain specialty items and high-quality supplements, provide a bit of emotional support, and recommend some healthy recipes.

I have also seen some dieticians and nutritionists offering assistance with grocery shopping trips as well as restaurant visits, actually accompanying clients during real-life experiences, which could be highly beneficial.

"The doctor of the future will no longer treat the human frame with drugs, but rather will cure and prevent disease with nutrition."

~ Thomas Edison

Chapter Fifty-Three

Natural Supplements

From all of the personal experience, my work with health professionals, information received from professional continuing education seminars, being Certified in Natural Holistic Remedies and a Certified Mental Health Integrative Medicine Provider, as well as extensive research, I have come up with a list of supplements that everyone should at least consider taking, especially if you have an illness (of course check with your healthcare professional first, and conduct your own research taking into account your specific health conditions). Although it is rare, there are medicine and supplement interaction precautions, therefore you will need to review those possibilities with your healthcare provider. Pharmacists can also sometimes answer questions. Remember to always start your supplements at low or infrequent dosages and increase as indicated (and as tolerated).

As you are reading through this section, an important thing to keep in mind was summed up by Anne Procyk, Naturopathic Physician, in a recent Continuing Education professional seminar:

"Nutritional supplements are never the full answer: they are supplements to a healthy diet."

Here is what I have found to be some key supplements to a nutritious diet, helpful to the healing process, and highly beneficial for a goal of overall health:

Omega-3 essential fatty acids are crucial to the health restoration process as well as health maintenance. High-quality fish oil seems to be the best form of Omega-3 supplementation for the majority of people. Omega-3s (EPA, DHA, and ALA) are great for heart health, brain function, mood, and much more. Cod liver oil provides Omega-3 as well as Vitamins D and A. Conditions that benefit from Omega-3s include RA, any type of inflammation, depression, and much more. Omega-3 plays an important role in balancing the immune system (such as what is needed for the treatment of autoimmune disorders). Algae oil is also an Omega-3 supplement option to consider. There are other additional plant-based sources of Omega-3. As far as all supplements go, many natural health professionals recommend beginning with Omega-3 supplementation as the most important and the base of healing (and you can add additional types of supplements later). Along these lines, my eye doctor is always quite pleased to hear about my taking Omega-3 as it is highly beneficial for eye health as well. She is a fan of the anti-inflammatory properties and how it relates to my needs. It also helps with issues such as dryness of the eye. Again, make sure your fish oil comes from a high quality source (it needs to say "molecularly distilled" for maximum purity). Anne Procyk, ND, recommended taking your Omega-3 supplement just before meals in order to minimize "fish burps" and to ensure proper absorption. Work with your healthcare provider and begin a "therapeutic dose", and then later on perhaps a lowered "maintenance dose" for more ongoing use.

I currently like Vita Breeze™ Omega 3 Fish Oil (the manufacturer is highly responsive to any questions). I have also heard from multiple trusted sources that the Nordic Naturals® brand is recommended as well. After you have completed both the therapeutic dose of Omega-3, and the subsequent maintenance doses, and you are feeling well, you may take breaks from Omega-3 supplementation. You may take long breaks if you are eating a variety of Omega-3 foods on a regular basis. For storage of Omega-3 supplements, always keep them in a cool dark place. Michael Lara, MD, has recommended storing them in the refrigerator. He also stated there is a "freezer test" where you can place them in the freezer and if they DO NOT freeze, that means they are still good. In addition, he said that if the supplement has a rancid smell, discard it as it is past its prime.

"I see Omega-3 as the off switch for inflammation."

~ Michael Lara, MD

Probiotics, "good bacteria", are also important for the healing process. There is increasing evidence confirming the connection between gut bacteria and physical as well as mental health conditions. Research is showing that some modern illnesses are linked to the loss of microbes, especially early in life. For just one example, scientists have recently associated the absence of four types of gut bacteria to asthma. There are also exciting new studies being done using probiotics as actual antibiotics! The use of certain probiotics to destroy pathogens is quite promising, but most of the work is still preliminary, according to scientists. The inclusion of "good bacteria" also seems to be part of every treatment plan for leaky gut syndrome and necessary during and after antibiotic use. In addition, probiotics actually play a role in balancing the immune system (also included in the treatment of autoimmune disorders). Remember that over eighty percent of your immune system is in your gut, and the more healthy good bacteria you have, the harder it is for disease-causing microorganisms to make you ill. Probiotics help restore your internal flora which improves your immune system naturally, increasing your digestive health, while controlling yeast overgrowth as well as providing relief from allergies, gas, and constipation. Poor overall health, an unhealthy immune system, and fatigue are often partly due to the gut not absorbing nutrients effectively. Probiotics can help the body absorb essential nutrients, increase energy levels, and assist with mental health (the gut is sometimes called the "second brain"). Taking probiotics regularly can actually improve digestion and intestinal track function. Optimizing your gut flora also helps ward off chronic inflammation. Many inflammatory diseases seem to begin in the gut, at least partly due to an imbalanced microbiome. Studies have also shown that improvement in gut function may help to increase metabolism and therefore assist in weight loss.

For your daily probiotic supplement, pack in as many strains as possible (however not too strong of a dose, especially at first, as too much can cause digestive upset or irritation, and other issues), along with assistance from your healthcare provider. Currently, in general, a high-quality supplement seems to be BioGanix® BIOPRO-50 Probiotic with 50 Billion CFUs and 11 Strains, available online. The manufacturer is quite helpful for any questions you may have. Swanson® Dr. Stephen Langer's Ultimate 16 Strain Probiotic is also a supplement to consider. Interestingly, it has been suggested by my colleagues specifically for the mental health benefits, and more. In addition, probiotics containing natural antifungal compounds have come to the forefront recently and are worth researching for your particular condition.

Note: I try not to order supplements such as probiotics online during hotter time periods as the product may lose some effectiveness during the shipping process. Therefore, I usually order in the springtime, or in cooler time periods, for future use.

"Probiotics are 'friendly' bacteria that may help you fight infections, boost your immunity, keep you regular, prevent harmful bacteria from growing in your stomach, and make B vitamins your body needs."

~ WebMD

L-Glutamine is another supplement to consider as it can be highly beneficial to the healing process. It is frequently used to assist in restoring intestinal health, among other uses. It is part of most treatment plans I have seen for leaky gut syndrome. Again, when the gut is healed, there is a much better opportunity for vibrant health to follow. L-Glutamine supplements are available online. There are some combinations that also contain some L-Glutamine so keep your eye out for those supplements. In addition, there are digestive enzyme brands that also contain it. This could be beneficial for those who have trouble digesting the protein. This way one can continue the gut healing process and the enzymes are sure to help the body process and absorb the L-Glutamine. If you do not have an enzyme and L-Glutamine combo in one supplement, and you have trouble digesting protein, then consider taking your L-Glutamine around the same time as your enzymes. It is important to note that some foods also contain L-Glutamine.

Vitamin D deficiency is linked to immune system problems (autoimmune diseases, possibly all of them, and other immune system issues).

Specifically, Vitamin D3 seems to be most important (therefore make sure you are getting enough of Vitamin D3). Absorbing sunlight can help as well, so head out into the sun whenever possible (as tolerated). Vitamin D helps regulate the amount of calcium and phosphorus in the blood, reduces inflammation and pain, supports immune function, helps the body heal, and more. Interestingly, depressed individuals generally have lower Vitamin D levels than non-depressed people. I currently take Vitamin D3, especially during the winter months. Recent research is also suggesting that it is beneficial to include Vitamin K2 with Vitamin D supplementation. In addition, make sure that magnesium levels are sufficient. Anne Procyk, ND, has said that it can be beneficial for many people to take Vitamin D year-round on an ongoing basis. She stated that Vitamin D toxicity is extremely rare and that there are many more risks associated with being on the low side. She recommended getting Vitamin D levels checked on a regular basis. My level has been low in the past, but lately, because of all the healing activities, it has been fine.

"Optimize Vitamin D. The best way to increase your Vitamin D is through sun exposure. If you live in a climate where you don't get enough sun, try taking a Vitamin D supplement. Optimal blood levels of Vitamin D are between 40-80 ng/ml. It generally takes 5,000 IU per day to maintain this level. You can get your level checked with a test kit from grassrootshealth.net."

~ **Christiane Northrup, M.D.**

B-complex vitamin supplementation is necessary for many people. Anne Procyk, ND, has strongly emphasized the importance of purchasing a "stress formula" with a balance of all the B-vitamins. She has stated that B-vitamins are used in countless biochemical reactions within the body related to energy production. She said that they are necessary for optimal adrenal function (handling stress) as well as neurotransmitter production. Also, according to her, the quality of a B-complex supplement is not quite as crucial as it is with fish oils, therefore it is much simpler, just make sure you are getting as many of the "B's" as possible in your supplement so as not to create an imbalance (of one type over another). Also make sure your supplement is natural and not synthetic. Remember that stress depletes B-vitamins from the body, which can contribute to a whole host of problems. Interestingly, studies have also been done to prove the benefits of riboflavin (Vitamin B2) therapy for migraines with positive outcomes! There is also research supporting the role of B-vitamins in brain health issues (such as Alzheimer's).

Magnesium deficiency is quite common and can cause a whole host of serious problems in the body, both physically and mentally. According to Anne Procyk, ND, magnesium is the most important nutrient for mental health, being critical for relaxation of nerve and muscle cells. She also stated that magnesium deficiency is almost always the cause of restless leg syndrome and medical doctors are finally starting to look to magnesium supplementation before pharmaceuticals for that condition. In addition, she said coupled with an unhealthy diet, too much calcium intake can cause magnesium deficiency. She recommended Epsom salt baths as one way to raise magnesium levels (safe for adults and children). Correcting a magnesium deficiency using Epsom salt baths can provide relief. The following are just a few symptoms of magnesium deficiency: agitation and all types of anxiety, insomnia, irritability and anger, nausea and digestive imbalance, abnormal heart rhythms, high blood pressure, heightened sensitivity to pain, muscle spasms, and restless leg syndrome. While magnesium supplements may be taken orally, other foods, drugs and certain medical conditions may also interfere with their effectiveness. Anne Procyk, ND, also stated that you should take magnesium supplements to what is called "bowel tolerance". This means that if you are taking magnesium and your bowels are beginning to be affected in a negative way for you, then decrease your dose. She also suggested taking magnesium glycinate when bowels are oversensitive, and magnesium citrate or magnesium oxide when constipation is an issue. I currently take magnesium lactate by Standard Process®, from my current acupuncturist, and have found it to work quite well in all ways.

Lithium in its natural mineral form is being used in the treatment of certain types of depression, mental health issues, and addictions. Additional benefits seem to include cognitive enhancement, decreasing inflammation, and lengthening circadian rhythm. Lithium Orotate seems to be the specific type in which to seek. Do not take while pregnant or nursing.

Calcium supplementation may also be necessary. However, do not take too much calcium, because as said, that can cause an imbalance in the body, such as magnesium deficiency. Also according to Anne Procyck, ND, there is building evidence that calcium supplementation over 500mg per day can increase the risk of heart disease. Work with your healthcare provider on this and also consider all of your calcium sources (including dietary as well as medication sources) to make sure you are not overdoing it. Make sure your calcium is a high-quality source. Many nutritional experts state that calcium carbonate is not usually absorbed well by the human body, therefore you may want to consider one or more of the following types of calcium instead: lactate, citrate, or orotate.

Zinc is a trace element essential for cells of the immune system, and zinc deficiency affects the ability of T cells and other immune cells to function properly. It is estimated thirty percent of Americans are deficient in this mineral needed for seventy enzymatic processes. Zinc is crucial for your digestive tract and one of the main functions is to help maintain intestinal wall integrity. Zinc supplementation has been shown to help in the healing of leaky gut syndrome. A word of caution: While it is important to have a sufficient amount of Zinc, too much can actually inhibit immune system functioning.

Vitamin C could be quite beneficial for to add for your healing and continued health. High-quality natural Vitamin C supplements are definitely best. However, I recommend not taking extremely high doses for long periods of time, as that can create problems. Please discuss with your healthcare professional any concerns in regards to Vitamin C supplementation.

Pay special attention to any vitamin or mineral that tests are showing you are lacking (or what your health professional may determine you need to add due to low intake with food, or what will help your particular condition). Note that even if you fall within the "normal" range, if you are low normal it is probably an issue that needs attention, so you will need to know where you fall on the spectrum of each test. Sometimes blood tests are not adequate or available for a certain nutrient. You might have to go by just symptoms or other assessment methods. Getting all the nutrients that you need for a healthy nervous system is imperative. This can make all the difference between being able to handle a certain amount of stress without breaking down versus rapidly experiencing health issues when faced with stress. While it is essential for your overall health that you eat a well-balanced and nutrient-dense diet, I believe it is also important for many people to take supplements in order to ensure adequate intake of necessary vitamins and minerals, especially during the healing process. That said, proceed with some caution as it is well known that consuming too much of any particular supplement can lead to unwanted side effects.

It is important to note that now there are ways to obtain medical tests (such as nutrient levels) without an order from a health professional. One company is called Genova Diagnostics® and the website currently is: gdx.net/patients. They test samples from hair, saliva, urine, and blood. Sometimes health insurance will pay for the tests. Another company is DirectLabs. For blood tests they connect with lab service providers such as Quest Diagnostics™. Insurance does not currently seem to cover tests done by DirectLabs, but that could change in the future.

Detoxification supplements can also be beneficial. These aid in the detoxification of the body (such as liver detoxifiers or liver supports) and are definitely worth researching. I currently like LES Labs® liver health, detoxification, and enzyme support supplement. All of the ingredients in this supplement could be highly therapeutic, as it can help with more than just detoxification. The manufacturer is also available for any questions. Taking this supplement on an ongoing basis is probably not recommended. Shorter-term time periods would probably work well, or during/after known exposure to toxins (or if there are possible liver health issues, or toxicity shows up in a blood or hair test). Silica is another supplement to consider taking for detoxification, especially from heavy metals. (See the "Detoxify the Body" chapter for more information on silica).

Turmeric has recently shown to be an effective anti-inflammatory for many people, therefore it is definitely something to consider for a supplement. It is also known to be detoxifier for the body. It is of course a spice that can be used in foods, and also in pill form. In supplements it is sometimes called curcumin or curcuma longa. Take turmeric with black pepper and some fat for maximum absorption. Keep in mind turmeric supplementation is not for everyone, and probably should not be taken on a long-term basis. Please do your research and also see later in this chapter about Th1 and Th2 dominance issues and how that relates to some supplements.

SAMe is used for depression, anxiety, attention deficit-hyperactivity disorder (ADHD), heart disease, fibromyalgia, chronic fatigue syndrome, Parkinson's, MS, osteoarthritis, bursitis, tendonitis, chronic lower back pain, dementia, slowing aging, improving intellectual performance, seizures, migraines, liver disease, spinal cord injury, and lead poisoning. The body uses SAMe to make certain chemicals in the body that play a role in the previous listed symptoms and conditions. People who do not naturally make enough SAMe will likely be helped by this supplement. SAMe is a chemical that is found naturally in the body and it can also be made in a laboratory. It has been available as a supplement in the United States since 1999, but it has been used as a prescription medication in Germany, Italy, and Spain. Researchers actually revealed the potential benefits of SAMe in treating osteoarthritis by accident. They were studying its effect on depression when the patients they were following also reported improvement in their osteoarthritis symptoms.

"Moducare", plant sterols and sterolins, by Throne Research®, is a supplement I currently take for immune adaptation (immune system balancing). I take it at bedtime as it has helped by calming down overactive aspects and creating more balance. It has been scientifically and clinically shown to stabilize (modulate) immune function and is a supplement to strongly consider if you have any immune system issues. It helps maintain a healthy balance of T-helper 1 and T-helper 2 white blood cells, and modulates a stress response by supporting optimal DHEA to cortisol ratios. DHEA is dehydroepiandrosterone which is a hormone produced by the adrenal glands.

Dermatrophin PMG® by Standard Process® is also a supplement I take, from my current acupuncturist, to assist with connective tissue disease (autoimmune) healing and health maintenance. This supplement contains protomorphogens (PMGs), which are truly fascinating and highly complex. I do not completely understand all the workings of PMGs and all they can do for the body and specific disorders, but I will provide a bit of information here, adapted from information received from my current acupuncturist. Protomorphology (the study of how PMGs work) has determined that PMGs are just bundles of enzymes and their activators. Enzymes are the key to growth, repair, and maintaining cell health. It is truly fascinating how cells inside embryos break off and differentiate into skin, hair, organs, and other cells. Inside each cell, we have hundreds of different enzymes, which are influenced by and responsive to nutrition, genetics, hormones, and the vibrations around us (including our thought processes). These PMGs act as one tool we can use in the healing process to provide a healthy genetic template or blueprint for cellular repair. PMGs promote healing over time. Protomorph products are composed of nucleus proteins and used to supply a better template so that the body can assemble available nutrients to repair damaged tissue in the glands being treated. PMG extracts were first invented by a dentist, Dr. Royal Lee, founder of Standard Process®, in the 1940's. He was a pioneer in the field of nutrition, far advanced when compared to anyone in his field during his time. PMGs are:

- Rebuilders: the mineral activators of a normal healthy mammal cell. Activators are needed to make a cell. It goes in and helps create a normal healthy cell.

- Buffers or decoys: Immune cells then start attacking the PMG molecules instead. This saves healthy tissue, rebuilding then occurs, and immune response gets modulated down.

Aloe Vera is another interesting supplement as it has seemingly countless healing properties. My goal with aloe for myself would be to support any additional healing of the gut, benefit immune system balancing, and increase overall health.

Digestive enzyme supplements can be an important addition as they assist the digestive process, leaky gut issues, immune system stabilization, and overall health. Consider including digestive enzyme supplements especially if you have any GI, nutrient absorption, or immune system concerns. I have been on enzymes in the past and have started to use them again (this time it is absolutely necessary due to a blood test confirming a difficulty processing protein, among other issues). There are numerous quality supplements available. The enzymes I currently take assist in the breakdown of a wide range of proteins, peptides, fats, complex carbohydrates, sugars, and fibers. Klaire Labs® brand has been good for me. Start enzymes "low and slow", first with your largest meal. As a general side note about enzymes, keep in mind there are many whole healthy foods which also contain them.

Again, I have personally found the following nutritional smoothie mix to be extremely helpful in restoring gut health as well as aiding in the detoxification process: MediClear Plus® by Thorne Research® (available online). This is a supplement to use just for shorter periods of time, not on an ongoing basis. There has also been a special diet to follow, associated with the smoothie mix, designed to help with detoxification, decreasing inflammation, healing gut issues, and decreasing allergies.

Gingko Biloba has been shown to reduce cortisol production in the body, which then contributes to overall health. Ginkgo extract is used medicinally to increase memory, energy, alertness, blood flow, sex drive, and more. It also helps protect against oxidative cell damage from free radicals, and has been used to treat a number of cardiovascular, renal, respiratory, and central nervous system disorders. Recent data suggests it can be an effective supplement to use for memory loss diseases, such as Alzheimer's.   It is an alternative to caffeine (which can actually increase cortisol levels).

5-HTP (also called 5-hydroxytryptophan or Oxitriptan) has been shown to increase brain dopamine and noradrenaline activity (essential mood and alertness-regulating neurotransmitters).   It can be beneficial for depression (including bipolar), anxiety, and hormonal mood swings.   Research suggests that 5-HTP is effective for depression that is more anxious, agitated, aggressive, or irritable.   5-HTP is a building block of serotonin, the "feel good" neurotransmitter that regulates moods, sleep cycles, and even influences response to pain.   It is known to increase relaxation and sleep, and can be a natural alternative to Prozac.   Preliminary evidence is also suggesting that supplementation with 5-HTP may promote weight loss by helping to reduce appetite, caloric intake, and "emotional" eating.   According to Anne Procyk, Naturopathic Physician, it has been useful in reducing withdrawal symptoms while weaning off of SSRI medications (but you absolutely have to work closely with your physician while weaning, and do not use 5-HTP while still on your full SSRI dose).   Always start 5-HTP at a low dose and increase as indicated.

St John's Wart supplementation has been shown to be effective for patients with mild depression.   Therefore it is a natural alternative to pharmaceuticals for treatment.   There are precautions to use with St John's Wart however, and you need to review all medicines and medical conditions with your healthcare provider (before and during the use of St John's Wart).

A few other supplements to fully research and possibly try:

• Feverfew is known for preventing or reducing pain and inflammation.

• NutriO2 is said to bring oxygen to the cells which aids the body in healing from a host of health conditions (including mental health).

- Cannabidiol (CBD) is beginning to show great promise in benefitting autoimmune patients and much more. CBD seems to tamp down an overactive immune system, allowing the body to be able to recognize the difference between normal anatomy and foreign invaders. It does not seem to produce psychoactive effects, has minimal side effects, is non-toxic, and non-addictive. As with all substances, make sure it comes from a trusted source to ensure authenticity, effectiveness, and purity.

- Thymus extract can help people who have any immune system-related issues. It has been known to help strengthen and balance the immune system.

- Licorice supplement is used for a variety of health issues such as stomach and intestinal problems, sore throats and coughs, pain and inflammation, skin disorders, hormonal imbalance, adrenal issues, as well as mental health concerns. It supports immune system health and also seems to have antimicrobial properties (including antiviral). Licorice supplementation really helps some people, but it is not for everyone. Please do your research and also be sure to read the information later in the chapter about Th1 and Th2 dominance issues. Some licorice supplements can also raise blood pressure, so if you are prone to that, it is something to take into consideration. It is highly recommended to consult with your healthcare provider to discuss any possible interaction or complications the use of licorice may cause in your particular case.

"As an antispasmodic, licorice can have an effect on cramps both abdominally and potentially in the muscles, as well. Topically, licorice can

alleviate eczema discomfort and other dermal conditions as it acts as a hydrocortisone. Anti-inflammatory benefits may also help relieve pain, including acting as a natural remedy for joint pain."

~ Dr. Josh Axe

Raw honey has been used since ancient times to treat multiple health conditions. My spiritual counselor suggested "supplementing" with raw Manuka honey due to its numerous therapeutic properties. Scientific research has actually confirmed several benefits, therefore it is definitely worth a try for many people. Of course, some may need to be careful with ingesting products like honey, and it is not suitable for everyone. However, raw Manuka honey is a rich antioxidant, with antimicrobial and anti-inflammatory characteristics. It can also help sleep and contains nutrients as well. When seeking Manuka honey it might be best to look for one that is UMF® certified (UMF 15+). The term UMF stands for Unique Manuka Factor, which is the phytochemical compound, derived from the Manuka bushes (tea trees), that gives the special properties, and is actually regulated by the Unique Manuka Factor Honey Association of New Zealand. Many certified Manuka products can be found online, such as "Kiva Certified UMF 15+ Raw Manuka Honey" by KIVA®. I have also started seeing them at supermarkets. Some say you absolutely have to use a "UMF certified" product in order to be guaranteed the therapeutic properties and others say to just make sure it is at least a "15" (such as Raw Manuka Honey by YS Eco Bee Farms). I will let you make that decision. The non-certified "15" products are usually much less expensive. I am currently using Manuka honey sparingly (I have replaced regular raw honey usage with Manuka honey due to the higher therapeutic benefits). I really enjoy it, but it probably is a bit of an acquired taste for some, and the aroma to me can be a bit like menthol. However, if it heals like many say it does, it is fine with me! Right now I am using a "250+" (but started with a "15+") and I have seen them up to "550+". Manuka honey is also used to treat various types of skin problems, as well as issues with teeth and gums.

Pau D' Arco is an herb to research and possibly add to your healing activities. Scientists have identified two active "chemicals" in it that have the power to kill bacteria, fungi, parasites, and viruses. They have also shown anti-inflammatory properties, which, as we know now, are important in treating numerous health conditions.

Marshmallow Root powder and Slippery Elm Bark powder are herbal supplements known for their "mucilage" content. Mucilage, when taken with water, forms a gel-like protective coating in the stomach and intestines, reducing irritation and inflammation. They promote healing in the entire GI tract and beyond.

Optimal Health Knowledge is a fascinating company that creates multiple nutritional supplements targeting cancer, GI issues, inflammation, and more. It is also worth a look!

DigestaCure® Autoimmune-X® by Pristine Nutraceuticals is another supplement to fully research and possibly try, for all autoimmune-related conditions, as it is recommended by Dr. Ronald P. Drucker (Natural Healing Practitioner).

- As far as other supplements, herbs, and remedies go, be sure to keep an open mind, do your research, and work with your healthcare professional. More ideas will then surface for you to try.

Test yourself first to see how you tolerate a certain supplement or activity. Start slow with a low and infrequent amount, then tweak as needed. Think positively but also be sure to listen to your body. It is also important to be open to switching to different brands, or changing the time of day you use them. Online there are many high-quality supplements, but it is important to at least consult with your healthcare professional about any regimen you are about to begin. Your provider most likely will have an understanding of what you need for your particular body, why, how much, and for how long you should take the supplement(s).

- Note that there are other chapters in this book that contain additional information on specific nutrients and their food sources.

PERQUE and Thorne Research® are examples high-quality supplement brands that I have used successfully, and many chiropractors seem to have in-office. They are available online now as well. I have heard Vital Nutrients® and Pharmax® being recommended from trusted sources as "high-quality for low cost" brands, therefore they are also worth researching. Your local health food store is another source for high-quality supplements (like the Fruitful Yield health food stores in my area). Chinese medicinal herbs are an option as well, as I have gotten some from my former acupuncturist who practices TCM. Many acupuncturists also have other natural supplements, in addition to herbals, available in-office. My current acupuncturist works with the Standard Process® brand, and they are quite thorough in what conditions they treat. They seem to provide a massive amount of interesting high-quality products. In addition, I have come across additional supplements and nutrients which aid specifically in the healing of the gut (which helps overall health).

Research what your needs are, review with your healthcare provider, and give them a try!

- Note that there are additional natural supplements and remedies mentioned in other chapters throughout this book.

It is important to mention that the website Examine.com gives evidence tables (and other valuable information) on commonly used supplements and their uses, and as of now, it is still free. The following is from their website: *"Examine.com is an independent encyclopedia on supplementation and nutrition. We are not affiliated in any way with any supplement company and we have a team of health professionals analyzing the full body of research. We currently have over 41,000 references to scientific research."* Another helpful website, ConsumerLab.com®, contains an independent, consumer-oriented, ranking system of major supplements by brand (at the time of this writing there is a small fee to use it). In addition, I suggest PeoplesPharmacy.com for natural remedies, nutrition information, and informative medical reports. Easy-immune-health.com contains countless amounts of highly useful information as well.

All of my research and experience has continually shown that the human immune system is extremely complex, and many supplements and herbal remedies can have powerful influences on it. Even some supplements whose stated purpose has nothing to do with immune response can substantially affect it. One primary balance point in the immune system is between T-helper cells type 1 and 2. Many times, autoimmune patients have either too much expression of Th1 cells, or too much expression of Th2 cells. Apparently, when the Th1 cells of the immune system are overactive, they tend to suppress the activity of Th2 and vice versa. These two components of the immune system need to function in a balanced relationship. In the case of autoimmune disease, imbalances can further what seems to be an attack on healthy tissue, therefore tending to exacerbate symptoms.

Some supplements have been found to be stimulants of either Th1 cells or Th2 cells. When autoimmune patients take these supplements, their diseases might improve, but they could also flare up. Therefore, keep in mind that Th1 or Th2 dominance is a problem for many autoimmune patients, so enhancing an already existing dominance is not usually a good plan (especially if it is on a long-term basis).

Knowing one's Th1 or Th2 dominance (some doctors seem to be able to test for this) and targeting with specific supplements in order to raise or lower Th1 or Th2 can be helpful to some, but it might not be the best and safest approach for everyone. If you do decide to go this route, make sure to use the help of a practitioner who is skilled at using this type of intervention.

Although there are exceptions, and more research needs to be done, some studies claim to show the conditions that have most commonly been associated with a Th1 or Th2 dominant state. If you decide to act on this, make sure the information you receive is from trusted sources, is current, and that you cross-check with as much research as possible, while working with your healthcare provider.

Even though some research has grouped certain conditions under either the Th1 or the Th2 categories, it is possible, however, for it to be the opposite, or to have both Th1 and Th2 simultaneously overactive or under-active. Pregnancy can shift the immune system, at least temporarily, to Th2. Exacerbated occurrences of Th2-associated conditions are seen in pregnancy, as it is a complex immunological state in which tendency towards Th2 actually protects the fetus. An essential prerequisite for a healthy pregnancy is that the maternal immune system does not reject the fetus, therefore down-regulation of the Th1 immune response could be necessary.

Again, if you suffer from autoimmunity, you might be overly sensitive to supplements that affect the immune system. Therefore, it is important for patients to be well-informed about which compounds stimulate Th1 and Th2 because of how they can improve or worsen symptoms and disease progression.

Some supplements/compounds/substances which may stimulate or increase Th1:

- Licorice root

- Ashwaganda

- Ginseng

- Immune-boosting medicinal mushroom extracts

- Chlorella

- Echinacea (stimulates the Th1 but can be somewhat of immune balancer and may stimulate Th2 at bit as well... Try the tea few times a week, maximum, if Th2 dominant, and see how you feel. I currently enjoy an occasional cup).

Some supplements/compounds/substances which may stimulate or increase Th2:

- Curcumin (derived from turmeric)

- Green Tea

- Black Tea

- Caffeine

- Coffee

- Resveratrol

- Pycnogenol

- Genistein (derived from soybeans)

Note that some of the above substances can have additional side effects (such as elevating blood pressure as just one example), therefore be sure to conduct your own research and work closely with your healthcare professional before starting any new supplements.

There are certain foods which are said to either stimulate the Th1 or Th2. Many of them are related to the supplements listed previously, as those compounds often contain concentrated forms of substances found in foods, therefore have a much stronger effect. So, first and foremost, make sure you are not taking a supplement that stimulates your immune system in a non-beneficial way. You can also then research which foods you might want to increase or avoid in order to stimulate or decrease the Th1 or Th2 (keeping in mind the concentrated forms, or in high amounts, have more of an effect). Be sure the information is taken from trusted multiple sources and that you still continue to listen to your body during the entire process.

It can be quite helpful for people with autoimmune diseases to support the production of Regulatory T cells. These are the cells that promote immune tolerance, which is the ability of your immune system to leave your own tissues alone, rather than what seems like an attack them. Regulatory T cells are a component of the immune system that suppresses immune responses of other cells to prevent excessive reactions. Regulatory T cells are involved in shutting down immune responses after they have successfully eliminated "invaders", and also in preventing autoimmunity. Therefore, Regulatory T cells play a significant role in suppression of autoimmune pathology. Some healthcare providers are able to tailor a program of Regulatory T cell support for each specific case.

Remember, it is balancing and creating a healthy immune system that is imperative, and a safe alternative seems to be focusing on compounds that have been shown to stabilize the immune system (meanwhile implementing other strategies mentioned in this book that have been shown to heal the body). We do know what can bring balance to the immune system for all (or most) people. Including Omega 3's, digestive enzymes, "good" bacteria, and supplements such as plant sterols/sterolins (the immune-balancing types), along with countless other lifestyle and behavioral change suggestions, all can help balance the entire immune system. This is can be highly beneficial for all (or most) health conditions. Certain therapeutic treatments and healing activities can also bring natural balance to the body. In addition, treating infections and toxicities, avoiding allergens, eating foods that are beneficial for your particular body/health conditions, and healing leaky gut syndrome, all will help tremendously. Keeping Vitamins D, A, and E, as well as all other nutrients at healthy levels is necessary as well. For additional support of your immune system, it is imperative that you avoid sugar (especially refined or processed sugars). Avoiding sugar is immune suppressive (in a beneficial way) and anti-inflammatory.

Colostrum (a mother's first milk that is actually available in supplement form) is also something that has been used for immune system balancing. In addition, as stated earlier, thymus extract is another supplement to consider researching for your particular condition.

Low glutathione in the body can cause the immune system to go out of balance. Glutathione is available in supplement form, however, I believe lifestyle changes are the best way to increase it in the body, first and foremost. Consuming a variety of fresh, organic produce is helpful in providing the body with the nutrients it needs to create glutathione. Sulfur-rich vegetables such as garlic, onions, parsley, and cruciferous vegetables can be particularly helpful in addition to avocados, squash, and tomatoes. Note that cooking reduces the glutathione content of vegetables, and canning seems to eliminate it. Stress depletes it in the body, and so does exceedingly strenuous exercise. This can all lead to extensive cellular damage as well as other problems. Therefore, be sure to practice healthy fitness and discover a balance that works for you, including always getting adequate rest and recovery time.

It is important to note that iodine supplements can possibly trigger or flare autoimmune diseases, especially Hashimoto's and Graves'. In the United States, a high amount of women with hypothyroidism actually have Hashimoto's. Therefore, adding iodine supplementation if you are hypothyroid could be risky. Again, I urge you to review all concerns with your healthcare provider and conduct your own research. This book contains a list of iodine-containing foods (which may enable you to get the iodine you need naturally, without supplementation).

With all that has been said here, I wanted to add an important quote from Michelle Corey, C.N.W.C., F.M.C. (Functional Medical Consultant, Nutritionist, and Author):

"...natural immune system modulators such as green tea, white willow, pycnogenol, reishi mushroom and echinacea may help many people feel better while they are healing, but they should not be used like pharmaceuticals to mask or suppress a natural response of the body to heal itself. A good practitioner will always start with removing pieces of the splinter. If she feels that calming the immune system at the same time will help you to feel better and heal faster, that's great...just make sure she's looking for the cause of the immune system flare at the same time!"

- Given all of the information thus far, always remember that in supplementation as well as diet, there is not usually just one panacea, and everyone is a bit different ~ Therefore, listening to your own body is key.

Having trouble taking supplement pills?

If you have difficulty swallowing pills, you are definitely not alone. There are many other options, so no worries! Almost all the supplements I currently buy are either in liquid, powder, or chewable form. There are some that are capsules which are easy to take apart and place into liquid. A few have been caplets but they are able to be crushed and dissolved into water, or chewed. Pill crushers can also be utilized. Just make sure it is okay to change the way to take a certain supplement (by checking with the manufacturer as well as your healthcare provider) and then you will be good to go! It is important to note that some supplements can also be topical, such as magnesium.

There is another benefit to not taking actual whole pills which is that starting out at a low dose first (recommended) is much easier to do that way.

Chapter Fifty-Four

Non-Toxic Cleaning Solutions and Remedies

D o you want to know about a non-toxic chemical-free disinfecting agent that works effectively on just about anything? The ingredients are half vinegar and half hydrogen peroxide (H2O2) (available at your local pharmacy). I use rice vinegar, but any other white vinegar can work, according to your preference. The concoction is always on hand in a spray bottle at my house. It is anti-microbial (kills bacteria, fungi, and parasites) and it also destroys viruses. It has been shown that the combination of H2O2 and vinegar (used as a spray mist) kills virtually all salmonella and E. coli bacteria on heavily contaminated food and surfaces. I use it on everything from cleaning fresh vegetables and fruits (rinse well with cold water after spraying), to almost all household uses. It has a bit of a strong smell, so try not to inhale while using. Also avoid spraying it on your skin. Be sure to research and spot-test first if you are concerned about a particular finish or material.

In my opinion, H2O2 is one of the absolute best cleaners and household remedies. It is safe, readily available, inexpensive, and effective! As far back as the early nineteenth century, H2O2 was actually widely used in medicine. Many bacterial diseases (including syphilis) responded to it when no other treatment was effective. In the early twentieth century, it was used to treat many common illnesses, such as whooping cough, ulcers, asthma, and tuberculosis. However, as the pharmaceutical industry began to develop synthetic new drugs (which could be sold for much more money), H2O2 unfortunately was increasingly overlooked and discarded as a treatment.

Interestingly, breast milk (especially colostrum) contains exceptionally high concentrations of H2O2. One of the functions of mother's milk is to activate and stimulate the immune system in the infant, therefore the fact that it contains large amounts of H2O2 makes sense.

H2O2 stimulates natural killer cells, which actually attack cancer cells as they attempt to spread in the body. In the body's immune response, H2O2 is released by T-cells to destroy invading bacteria, fungi, and viruses. Blood platelets release H2O2 on encountering particulates in blood. In the large intestine, acidophilus lactobacillus produces H2O2 which helps keep Candida yeast from multiplying. When Candida spreads out of the intestines, it seems that it can gain a foothold in other organs of the body, which many say is actually the cause of some diseases.

During the cold and flu season, if you feel like you are getting sick, try putting a drop of H2O2 into your ear. After a few seconds, the liquid will bubble, indicating that it is stopping infection. After approximately five minutes, drain and repeat in the other ear. If tolerated well, next time try two drops in each ear. I do this when a cold virus is keeping me awake and it usually tamps down the symptoms, so I can get some sleep.

The complete workings of H2O2 are not yet fully understood, but we do know it is full of oxygen. When it is taken into the body (orally or intravenously), the oxygen content of the blood and tissues increases. Note that the H2O2 available at your local pharmacy (3% hydrogen peroxide) should not be ingested orally, as it contains many stabilizers. The only grade suggested for internal use is 35% Food Grade Hydrogen Peroxide, which must be properly diluted down to 3% with water.

H2O2 can also be used as a natural "bleach" to whiten clothes, as a remedy for foot fungus, as a nasal spray to fight sinus infections (review with your health professional first and follow all directions), as an effective and inexpensive mouthwash/natural teeth whitener, and along with baking soda for natural toothpaste (again, review with your dental professional and follow all directions before using H2O2 orally).

Be sure to keep your H2O2 away from light (store in a cabinet or under the sink). It breaks down when exposed, which is why it is packaged in the opaque containers.

As mentioned earlier, using only chemical-free cleaning, household, and personal care products will go far in decreasing your toxic load and calming down your immune system. To obtain a list of some of my personal favorite products and brands, please feel free to email us at: gs@ginaspielman.com. We will be happy to provide the information.

Also consider plain old pure baking soda for any of your cleaning, deodorizing, or personal care needs.

I just have to mention that along the lines of household uses, Norwex® has an amazing window cleaning system, using just water and their special cloths. In addition, a simple blend of white vinegar, witch hazel astringent, and warm water shines up my wood floors and all of the glass in my house quite nicely!

Chapter Fifty-Five

TV and Movies

You will probably discover that the types of television shows and movies you enjoy watching will change as you begin to recover and have more positive energy. I think most comedy shows can be beneficial, as well as movies which are thought-provoking and educational. If a program helps you identify, express, and release your own feelings about a certain issue, it can also be therapeutic. However, be careful of traumatic, violent, or stressful shows or movies. Pay attention to how your body feels when you watch certain programs and turn it off if you are feeling too much negative energy. If you are not able to change the program, then make sure you do not allow the negativity to enter your mind or body. Imagine rising above or distancing yourself from the trauma, violence, or stress, while keeping the positive energy running throughout your body. Again, always make it known that any "bad vibes" do not have a "home" with you.

"Good things start to happen when you distance yourself from the

negativity"

~ Billy Cox

One (among many) movies I suggest watching is "The Secret". It includes in-depth comments (by authors, psychologists, physicians, financial professionals, a therapist, an entrepreneur, a visionary, a philosopher, and a quantum physicist) on an exploration of the power of positive thinking (and feeling), and how it can be used with the Law of Attraction to attain health, wealth, love, and happiness. There is also a book available (same title). I truly believe that working "The Secret", which I began years ago, helped bring exactly what I needed in order to restore health. It did take many years to be fully complete, but it did happen. Work it, show the Universe that you are taking the steps, be patient, and watch it unfold!

I have recently found several fascinating documentaries to watch on our paid movie program we have at home, and have learned quite a bit watching those. Of course you cannot and should not believe everything you hear or see on television, because there are so many contributing factors for one particular issue, but much of what I have watched and learned thus far has seemed to add significantly to my health.

Chapter Fifty-Six

Be Careful of "Internet Research"

Please be cautious looking up disease information on the internet especially if you are newly diagnosed. Typically what I have found is that many internet sites (even the most reputable ones) show the worst case scenarios. Often there are "delightful" pictures included (as in my experience looking up certain autoimmune disorders). I do not know who typically is responsible for writing these types of articles, but it usually seems like they are geared toward medical professionals only. They are often not patient-friendly, and little thought has been given to how a newly diagnosed person might feel after seeing the information.

If you find yourself in this type of unfortunate situation, seeing disturbing information on the internet, immediately think of all the people you know who have healed from serious illness or are at least in remission (or functioning well) after being diagnosed with what was thought to be a devastating disease. This will help you snap out of fear mode and back into healing mode. Assigning a trusted friend or family member to do most of the research for you can allow the receiving of needed information without experiencing the trauma of seeing the worst case scenarios first hand. Therefore, if friends or family members are asking "How can I help?" this may be one way they can assist you significantly.

Chapter Fifty-Seven

Information from Melissa J. Roth, Hypnotherapist

Questions and answers from a hypnotherapist who has had a high success rate in reducing symptoms in patients with physical conditions:

Her answers to my questions are in italic:

What are all the different autoimmune diseases you have treated with hypnosis? Are there other medical diagnoses you have treated with hypnosis (such as cancer)?: *There are way too many to list. The most recurrent ones I have seen are MS, rheumatoid arthritis, fibromyalgia (I don't qualify FMS as autoimmune but the rest of the internet does), diabetes type 2, chronic fatigue, Crohn's, many dysautonomias, immune deficiencies). Then there are all the rare ones physicians have gotten me to help in diagnosing.*

All I do is medical applications of hypnotherapy: IBS, fibromyalgia, pain control, migraines, hypertension, asthma, cancer, all kinds of undiagnosed/undiagnosable illnesses, thyroid diseases, and whatever else the docs send over. All my clients are referred by their physicians. I don't do smoking, weight, stress or broken hearts, only medical issues that have not responded to allopathic medicine or not responded well enough for the client to actually feel better.

Do you call it a cure, remission, healing, or reversal?: *I only talk about symptom relief. It's my personal belief that the human body comes with a very powerful self healing system already installed. As a hypnotherapist it is out of my scope of practice to talk about "cure" or "healing", etc. Yes, several MD's have sent me clients and asked for help in diagnosing what's going on with them. I usually communicate my findings for them to check out. We work as a team for the client. And, if I think the client needs a specific drug or some other therapy (massage, acupuncture, etc) or treatment, I'll communicate that to the referring MD.*

Do you consider "no symptoms" as a complete success of your treatment, or do you want to see actual results such as in blood tests?: *My clients want relief from the symptoms of their disease. I want to eliminate the disease altogether. So, the first thing I do with anyone is give them symptom relief. Most of my clients are so impressed with the ability to get relief from using hypnosis that they stick around for us to work on eliminating their illness from the body. And, in many instances we do. I had one woman who had suffered with worsening MS for approximately 12 years. On one of her sessions she came in very upset. She had just come from her neurologist's office. Her neurologist had just taken her off all her MD meds stating there were no longer any lesions. I was thrilled that there were no new lesions. She corrected me that there were NO lesions left--not just new ones. But, I noticed she was not happy. So, I asked her if she needed MS for any reason and she responded that there were 2 major situations in her life that were not quite finalized yet. So, I gave her suggestions that she could keep all the problems she needed until both events occurred. I saw a mutual friend a few months ago and she said the client was out of her braces and doing well.*

The best part of most of these therapies is that the symptoms do not return when the sessions end. The client keeps whatever gains they have made. Depending on the illness and client some people do not become completely symptom free. There's a variety of reasons for that. However, for most of the issues I see (IBS, Fibro, pain, migraines) the client becomes symptom free over 85% of the time and the symptoms do not return when the sessions end. I have tracked and kept records on clients since 1996. For IBS, 86% of clients will become and remain symptom free. Fibro 82%, migraines 90+%, chronic pain over 90%. Sorry, I have not kept records on other illnesses but most become and remain symptom free.

Does the patient have to continue working on certain things throughout lifetime in order to keep illness under control ongoing?: *I encourage clients to keep follow up sessions every 6 months or so. Some do. Most don't. Yet, when we contact them they are still symptom free. I tell them, "Good grief, you change the oil in your car every once in a while. Do something positive for your body every so often and keep it running well."*

How long does it typically take to successfully treat a disorder?: Time frames? *It's dependent on the illness. IBS is 6-8 sessions depending on age only, not severity of symptoms or length of time they have been ill. Fibromyalgia is a 12 session therapy. Most autoimmune diseases take an average of 12 sessions. Chronic pain typically is 3-5 sessions. Migraines are usually 2 sessions and I've never seen someone over 5 sessions for a migraine.*

Are there any cases where you and the patient did everything possible but not much progress took place?: *Yes, I've had failures just like everyone else. But, you don't want to be around me for a good month after a treatment failure. I just don't seem to let them go. I keep trying to figure out what went wrong, why they didn't get the outcome they wanted. It drives me crazy. Thank goodness my overall success rate is above 80% across the board so I'm not a grump too often.*

Can you give me an example of one of the top hypnosis scripts you typically use for this type of hypnosis (such as: "My healing has been accelerated")?: *They depend on the illness we're working on. I do not give any direct suggestions. I use metaphors and some NLP processes blended in. In one session for hypertension (strikes 90% of people over 50 years) I talk about rafting down a river (when I lived in the deep south I did a lot of white water rafting). Sometimes the current is nice and steady and it's fun to just lay back and enjoy the trip. But, sometimes the walls of the river bank get steep and narrow and the current gets dangerously fast. You must pay attention to prevent an accident and steer carefully. But, when the river walls broaden and flatten out the current becomes slower and more comfortable, less dangerous.*

For broken bones I talk about how roads are built with layer upon layer of varying size rocks and sand. How they are laid down upon each other before being coated with a smooth layer to travel upon and then sealed.

Have you had anyone with scleroderma?: *Yes, I have had one client with scleroderma. She was progressing well until she left the country and therefore ended therapy. I suggested online video sessions but she was not in a place where she had internet or cell phone service. And, yes, I have a book that is called "Taming The Chronic Illness Monster" that is how to work with autoimmune diseases. And, yes, when you have 1 autoimmune disease you usually have multiple. They like to keep each other company.*

We were making progress with the scleroderma before the sessions ended. The client had gotten at least a 50% reduction in Reynaud's, improvements in the areas of increased energy levels and declining levels of inflammatory markers. We did a session asking the unconscious mind what both triggered this illness and what was supporting its continuation? The unconscious mind answered and the client acknowledged she believed it was the correct answer. However, she was uncomfortable dealing with that answer. I believe that is why we did not make greater progress and that, if and when, she is comfortable addressing the answer we got then she can eliminate the scleroderma from her body.

What are the top dietary changes you recommend to your clients?: *Eliminate junk food and fast food COMPLETELY. I ask people to eat a low simple carb diet. They can have meat, fish, chicken, fruits (hopefully fresh or at least packed in their own juice) and veggies. They are asked not to drink fruit juices because they are mostly sugar and, therefore, high in simple carbohydrates. Most complex carbs are okay. Also, eliminate corn products because they exacerbate pain levels.*

Personally, I eat organic and non-GMO. In my opinion, gluten really isn't a problem except for the few people who have celiac disease. The reason wheat is a problem in the US is because it is sprayed with a potent herbicide prior to harvest. Spraying increases yield and makes harvest much easier and quicker. But, it is highly toxic and is linked to Non-Hodgkin's Lymphoma. Wheat in Europe does not cause gut problems because it is not sprayed with the herbicide prior to harvest. The EU banned it.

What do you think causes autoimmune diseases?: *I'm not a big fan of the genetic pre-disposition theories. Some illnesses are hard wired to your genes. However, most aren't. Read Bruce Lipton's "Biology of Belief" and Dawson Church's "The Genie in Your Genes". It is my personal belief that most autoimmune diseases are triggered by environmental pollution, exposure to toxic substances, GMO's, etc. In other words, my belief system is that most, not all but most, autoimmune diseases are triggered by environmental factors.*

If you got a diagnosis in less than 3 years of physician visits you are ahead of the curve. Getting a diagnosis is extremely difficult for most of the people I see as clients. They have suffered for years with no correct diagnosis. Almost all of them have been labeled as hypochondriacs (at best and usually worse). Then, once identified, treatment options are few and far between. But you have to remember the entire medical model is based on easing suffering for various illnesses. It does not cover wellness or return to wellness at all. That's not a slam on the healthcare system. Instead, it's an explanation for why it fails so many people. People are seeing doctors for all the wrong reasons. Also, you have to understand that the current medical system is funded by the pharmaceutical industry. The majority of the budget for the FDA is funded by Big Pharma. And, most medical schools in the US would have to close their doors if Big Pharma withdrew its funding. So, we have the best medical system the pharmaceutical industry can afford. But, its emphasis is not on health or wellness. That's precisely why the entire complimentary medical field has come into existence. People know that allopathic medicine has failed them and they are looking for relief and being restored to wholeness. Those are things allopathic medicine is not designed to do.

I just ran into another autoimmune client last weekend. She proudly informed me that after 24 years of allopathic medicine treatments for Lupus, after our sessions she was told she had never had an autoimmune disease. There were no disease markers left in her body. So, her new rheumatologist concluded that they must have made a mistake and misdiagnosed her with Lupus all those years ago and everyone else she has seen in the meantime was wrong also. He stated she never had Lupus because you can't just make it go away and she didn't have markers in her blood work and imaging studies. She didn't care if they thought it was a misdiagnosis as long as it wasn't causing her trouble anymore.

Do you offer online video sessions for those who are not in your area?: *Yes, I can work by online video sessions (I also do small groups and teach classes online). However, I require a medical referral before the sessions. They can email it (or mail it) if they are at a distance. But, I want to make sure an MD has ruled out all the other life threatening conditions that have the same symptoms as the autoimmune disease they come in with. I do not want to be working on eliminating rheumatoid arthritis to find out the client has cancer instead. Physicians are fallible and make incorrect diagnoses all the time. But I want to make sure exactly what the problems are the client is dealing with.*

I have home study training programs for other hypnotists. I also teach workshops in-person sometimes and at 3 conferences a year. For individuals who cannot see anyone I have trained, I have self-hypnosis programs on my website. So far, I have resisted those who want me to sell the therapy CD's individually. Currently I only sell them in complete sets because that is the way they work. Websites promising one session relief for things like fibromyalgia are, in my opinion, unethical. But, you can find both products for professionals and clients on my website, melissaroth.com.

The following had been obtained from Melissa Roth's website:

"Melissa Roth Hypnotherapy has a goal for our clients – that they become as comfortable, happy and healthy as possible-mentally, physically and emotionally. We help our clients achieve this through a series of hypnotic coaching sessions. We utilize a combination of hypnotherapy, NLP, energy techniques and health information and education. Just as each client is a unique human being our approach is tailored to the individual and their specific needs. Our therapies are not a substitute for conventional medicine. We are not opposed to conventional Western medicine. We simply want to make pharmaceutical agents unnecessary for most people and to enhance their benefits for those who are not being totally successful in easing their discomforts. And, we want to ease the suffering of those individuals for whom Western medicine does not have a solution. According to the World Health Organization, approximately 75% of all pharmaceutical agents are consumed in the US. In spite of that, we are among the most unhealthy individuals in the world. To me, that calls for a new paradigm in our approach to health and healing, a new paradigm that embraces what will work best for the individual. Hypnotherapy and hypnotic coaching represents an effective and short term approach to enhance mental, emotional and physical health. As a result of healing herself of both debilitating Irritable Bowel Syndrome and Fibromyalgia using self hypnosis, Melissa Roth became a clinical hypnotherapist specializing in medical applications of hypnotherapy. She first founded Alabama Hypnotherapy Center in Birmingham, Al. in 1995 and relocated to Boulder, Colorado Hypnotherapy in 2011. She continues to develop techniques and protocols to relieve the suffering of people experiencing illnesses and chronic conditions for which conventional medicine has little to offer."

Melissa J. Roth, Hypnotherapist   (Colorado)

Chapter Fifty-Eight

Tai Chi

Tai Chi practitioners know that they experience better overall health, but "how" is not always easy to explain, especially to westerners. Dr. Peter Wayne, an assistant professor at Harvard Medical School is inclined to believe that movement, breathing, attention, visualization, and rich psychosocial interactions, make Tai Chi a powerful tool for improving overall health.

According to research studies, Tai Chi can be a powerful force in improving immune system functioning. It seems that practicing Tai Chi creates more efficient, deeper breathing and increased blood circulation, allowing antibodies and cellular components of the immune system to better reach pathogens and neutralize them.

The following educational information was received from my friend and colleague Racquel Valencia Hays, who is a Licensed Clinical Social Worker and a Certified Alcohol and Drug Counselor. Currently, she has a private psychotherapy practice in Mount Prospect, Illinois, and is an adjunct faculty at

Wright College, one of the City Colleges of Chicago. She holds a brown belt in Tai Chi.

In the west, Tai Chi has largely been known as a stress management tool for seniors, but it is actually for all ages. Experience the flowing movements of Tai Chi and treat your whole body to a gentle and relaxing workout.

Say goodbye to sweating, puffing and panting. Say hello to feeling cool, calm, refreshed and energized.

Just 10 minutes a day is your passport to better health, fitness, peace of mind and so much more, as your mind and body work in harmony for superb results.

The core of your chi is in the dan tien. Chi is life force or energy. It's abundant in your body but it's up to you to be able to harness this through discipline and hard work. Tai Chi could be easy or hard but as my "FUSIFU" says, "it's about your state of mind....it's 80% mental, the rest is physical". Tai chi could be learned through "Sifu's" or "Masters" in a dojo (training class). This is more akin to the principles of martial arts. Some people can practice and learn the basics of Tai Chi in park districts or wellness centers but they may not offer a series of "promotions" to test your skills in the martial arts. Regardless, what is most important is gaining a foundation working with a "Master" whom you trust and can lead you to the right path and discipline.

This discipline rests in certain philosophies on how you value yourself, and the way you deal with opponents or challenges (metaphor). An example: if you have an opponent, you don't block your opponent, you get closer to him or her and you deflect the punches to the energies in which they are directed (going with the flow). But you must have discipline and balance to do this correctly. The discipline is being aware of your opponent's movements and sensing when the hit is going to take place.

Once a dojo is found, one should be trained under a master who can guide through the next series of movements which is meditation. It begins with the breath, and learning proper posture and stance. Movements are slow, methodical and easy on the cardio, but it's harder on the mind as it tests your patience, perseverance, and persistence. After months of practice, the payoff is worth it! We take breathing for granted but it is what gives our bodies vitality. Breathing properly can give us energy for the rest of the day or the impetus to discharge our negativity away. Breathing is taking in the full air into your dan tien (this is a spot an inch below the navel) and breathing out through the nose.

Incrementally, one can then begin to learn how to do a "standing meditation"; the beginning stages where balance is taken into account. All of Tai Chi is balance and learning to use your body while keeping the Chi going. What is significant about this is how your legs, arms, neck, feet, toes and abdomen are all integrated with the meditation. This is where the mind can clearly begin to be at rest, always present and responding to the movements of your body. The benefit of standing meditation is multifold: relaxation, mind body connection, stress reduction, exercise and discipline. It also tests your memory, and with enough practice, your sense memory will kick in and it becomes second nature!

The next stage is the 24 movements. It's universally practiced in dojos throughout the world! The 24 movements is synchronous with as many people trained in Tai Chi. This is the basic movements and it is integrating self-defense, balance, martial-arts and dance all at the same time. It's the most beautiful form of movement and expression that one can easily learn. 24 movements can be done in about 10 minutes. It is advisable to do this every day if possible. 24 movements can lead you to other, more complicated forms if one is interested in getting promoted to receiving a belt.

Anyone can learn this movement (all ages). We need to make it more accessible for all ages and not think that our seniors should be the only ones benefitting. This is a mistake! This form of wellness exercise is good for you physically, emotionally, mentally and spiritually!

PHYSICAL BENEFITS: My bones used to make sounds when I moved my hands, torso, arms or legs. After months of Tai Chi, this is not an issue. I used to have aching bones and muscles. After learning how to move with proper posture and balance, it is not much of an issue.

EMOTIONAL BENFETIS: When I learned how to do the meditation and movements, I used this several times before I would present in front of people. This has helped me eliminate nervous energy and anxiety.

COGNITIVE BENEFITS: Tai Chi has helped me with focus, discipline and memory skills.

PERFORMANCE BENEFITS: I have used the breathing meditation with many of my clients, and with the students in the college where I teach. Most have reported feeling more positively about themselves and it has calmed them down significantly.

SPIRITUAL BENEFITS: What I derive out of Tai Chi is a sense of love for oneself and others, especially when I've managed to accomplish another belt in my repertoire. There is camaraderie amongst the students. I have love and respect for my "FUSIFU" and the "GRAND MASTER" (owner of the dojo). My "FUSIFU" is a medical doctor and there is a compassion about him— a calming, healing presence and support that I've been extremely lucky to have in my life!

Chapter Fifty-Nine

Information from a Woman with Lupus

Below is an educational interview with a woman who had been diagnosed with lupus. Her name and identifying information will remain anonymous.

Her answers to my questions are in italic:

What factors which you think contributed to the diagnosis?: *I was sick for some time with an on-going low grade fever. For a few months. I saw several doctors and had a lot of blood tests but didn't get any answers. I finally went to see a doctor who came highly recommended by a friend. After thorough questions she said I had one of two things, one of which was lupus. She referred me for blood work and to see a rheumatologist. I couldn't get in to see the rheumy for weeks and did online research which was probably a mistake. By the time I saw him my stress had completely exacerbated all my symptoms. He confirmed lupus based on my symptoms and a positive ANA blood test. He recommended prednisone, which from all my research I wanted to avoid. He told me "good luck" with my choice of taking only an anti-inflammatory. Again, my symptoms were right on target with several lupus markers due to the stress. I became depressed and my primary then put me in an antidepressant and within a couple of weeks my symptoms were pretty much gone. I discontinued the antidepressants due to undesirable side effects.*

You had said that you tested negative after some time. How did you then test negative (what are all the things that you think contributed to testing negative)?: *I had to get tested every few months to check liver function (my lupus is systemic) and I would have to say the ANA was what the doctors would use to determine the lupus was still active. I believe it was positive for some years. At some point I did test negative for a few years. However it's important to note that I often had extended low-grade temperatures when I was "negative". I try not to think about it and try to live as healthy a lifestyle as possible. Eat clean, work out.*

Recently you indicated that you tested positive again. What do you think contributed to testing positive again?: *In the last year I tested positive again. I don't really have any symptoms other than the positive ANA. I occasionally run a temp. I think this is completely random and possibly (in my case) hormonally driven. I am going through menopause and my hormones are in flux, so I believe that's why it's positive again.*

Did you make key diet, lifestyle, and spiritual changes that significantly contributed to your healing?: *Not sure how spiritual this will be, but not clinical either. When I was diagnosed it was a tough time. My marriage was not in a good place. I felt like the loneliest married person ever. I suspected my (now ex) husband was unfaithful and our relationship was barely even friendly so I felt very alone. I remember asking him "what if this means I'm going to die" and he said something like "we'll deal with that if it happens" and turned away. He had other plans. I was certainly in a dark lonely place. My kids were young as I was dealing with the lupus. My parents each had cancer surgeries, one after the other. In fact my mom couldn't be with my dad for his surgery because she was going thru chemo, so I was there with him. Thankfully they are both still with us. So I didn't have the support of a spouse, my brother was living in Florida and my folks both had their own battles. Friends often don't deal well with serious health issues. Especially vague ones, right? I always tell people never minimize the effect of stress on your health.*

As for nutrition, I think I was diagnosed the same time StarLink was "accidentally" introduced into the human food system. I was also working in a facility where you could SMELL the chemicals in the air. Environmental factors are key. Now I buy organic as needed (most fruits and veggies), coffee and what limited dairy we consume. I only buy organic of the GMO crops if at all. If not organic then I buy non-GMO (lots of choices) whenever possible. I bake my own bread. I really minimize processed foods unless I've sourced them. For example I trust Trader Joe's. We eat mostly (low-mercury) fish, lots of fruits/veggies, and no soda. We don't eat out much.

As soon as I was diagnosed I started taking a mega-vitamin. Of course some research suggests it'll kill me but I've stuck with them. A natural form of "e" has helped me avoid those hot flashes thus far. Due to studies suggesting that dairy actually strips calcium from your body I take supplements and have all but given up on dairy. I'm doing research on gut health and probiotics.

Sleep can be difficult but I try to make that a priority. I've found that audio books (the same ones over and over by a narrator I find particularly soothing) will lull me to sleep or put me back to sleep at 2 a.m. Nice trick, works for me at least!

As I said I try not to think about it. For years I didn't even want to talk about it, it just upset me which could trigger a flare. The rheumy told me my systemic lupus was a "connective tissue disease" and that it could evolve into RA or MS. Of course being systemic I also need to check regularly for liver function etc. I eventually got comfortable with it. It's certainly hereditary, well at least my cousin has it bad, so if not hereditary your chances of getting it are greater percentage-wise. I read that mild lupus could burn out by menopause, which supports the hormone theory.

Late 40s were tough. I gained quite a bit of weight (thyroid, estrogen changes, etc). I warned my sister-in-law and now a few years later she's dealing with the weight gain, complaining of turning into a marshmallow. Now, she's active, fit and eats clean. I said "Who warned you!" and she said "You did".

Anyway, I do work out faithfully and rigorously. At diagnosis I was hardly able to walk through a retail store. Now lots of cardio and my resting and recovery heart rates are excellent. I enjoy the benefits of strength training, with a focus on core and balance. With the running I've finally added impact which is so important for menopausal bone health. Exercise is stress relief for me, thankfully, and when stress increases I turn up the dial on my workouts.

So again I'm not sure how "spiritual" this had been. I'm a practical kind of gal. I believe I am proactive about my health. I don't believe government/FDA/controlling industries have my best interests in mind. I do believe that you are what you eat. That's my best defense (that and staying strong physically). I am learning to love myself more and to not engage with (or at least limit exposure to) people who are toxic, also recognizing that other people's limitations are not a reflection on who I am.

Chapter Sixty

Another Highly Recommended Healing Activity

The following is another useful healing activity I definitely recommend adding to what you are already practicing now. Read it to yourself out loud, and write it down every day possible. Put some of the statements on sticky notes and post them all around the house, in the car, in your calendar, and so on. Alter them as needed tailoring to your specific needs.

This powerful activity originates from Anita Moorjani, the author of the amazing book "Dying to Be Me: My Journey from Cancer, to Near Death, to True Healing":

"When you wake up tomorrow morning, I want you to pretend that the doctor has just given you a clean bill of health. You have a fresh start. How does it feel? Get into that feeling, and go out and celebrate!! Wake up every day with that feeling, and celebrate life again. Live like a well person, who has everything to live for, and find joy in life again, and

excitement and passion. Live for the moment, and don't try to figure out the whys of what you have been going through. Don't replay them in your mind over and over, and don't worry about how it happened. Just find joy right now in this moment! Sending you love and healing!!"

Chapter Sixty-One

What Else Helps You?

What are all the activities you have found that improve your health and wellbeing? Relaxing while drinking herbal tea? Watching comedy? Listening to certain types of music? Following meditation or uplifting CD's? Working with a mindfulness app? Watching healing videos? Immersing yourself in the life-changing teachings of Quantum Physics? Practicing iRest Yoga Nidra? Doing Pilates? Dancing? Gardening? Coloring in an "art therapy" book? Making crafts and being creative? Whatever it is, identify what else helps, and do everything within your power to make time and participate in those activities as much as possible! Put yourself first and always remember that you deserve self-nurturing. It is absolutely necessary for your healing and continued wellness.

"To find what you seek in the road of life, the best proverb of all is that which says: "Leave no stone unturned".

~ **Edward Bulwer Lytton**

Keep in mind that what you focus on will likely increase. Continuing to shine a spotlight on positive things, what you want, and what you love will bring more of the same back to you again and again. Learn how to love your life, because it is essential in order to regain and maintain your health. Love this life!

Chapter Sixty-Two

"Abundance Comes to Me"

I know by now some of you are having thoughts such as "How am I ever going to pay for all the things I need for my healing?" I completely understand. However, I suggest you change those thoughts to affirmations such as "Abundance comes to me and I allow it". Also remember that some of the ideas in this book are completely free, so if you must begin with those, go for it! The free (and low cost) healing activities are sure to keep you busy for quite a while.

"Do what you can, with what you have, where you are".

~ Theodore Roosevelt

It is true that some of the activities, treatments, supplements, books, personal care items, and quality foods will cost money. I urge you to look at it as an investment in your health! I believe that following the recommendations in this book that resonate with you will not only bring more overall life satisfaction, but it is also likely to significantly lower your future medical bills. Not to mention decreasing the risk of lost wages due to being unhealthy and unable to work. In addition, the information in this book has the potential to help you live much longer. That is all well worth it in my opinion! Make sure your loved ones know everything you need, as well as where one can obtain those items or services. Perhaps you will then get them as gifts, or in the form of much-needed gift cards. What I have done, since beginning to need the suggestions in this book, is ask the Universe for the continued wealth and abundance to come to me (or my family) in order to pay for the services, special foods, supplements, and so on.

I encourage you to consider all of your possible options for additional income, and ways to obtain what you need. Be sure to continually ask yourself questions such as one that Michael Golzmane, Spiritual Clearing and Healing Facilitator, has suggested: "How can I be of service to others using my unique divine giftedness?" Only you can truly answer that question. When you do find the answers, be sure to take the necessary action steps and continually put yourself out into the world serving those needs, meanwhile being sure to keep your "receiving lines" open. After some time, you will likely find yourself in a situation of gainful "employment" that resonates with you.

Daily Affirmation: "*My income is constantly increasing. I am worthy of prosperity and abundance.*" Louise Hay

As far as other avenues of assistance, is there a family member who could help out temporarily, for such an important cause? Do you belong to a church that might be able to assist in some way? Is there any possibility to barter for any of your needed services? Negotiation can also be an option. The "abundance" will either begin to come to you quickly or after a bit of time. Be patient and keep continuing with your affirmations, and other activities such as clearing blockages, as you await the goodness that is coming to you.

"Acknowledging the good that is already in your life is the foundation for all abundance".

~ Eckhart Tolle

Again, I frequently say the mantra "Abundance comes to me and I allow it", including how amazing it feels to have goodness coming in and how thankful I am to be receiving it. I include how happy and grateful I am for all that I currently have and continually receive. Make it present tense and really feel the gratitude. As a result of thinking, saying, writing, and feeling these types of affirmations religiously, along with other suggestions in this book, I can truly say that I am able to continually obtain the things I need, and feeling grateful indeed!

"Daily Affirmation: MONEY is flowing to me from both EXPECTED and UNEXPECTED sources".

~ John Assaraf

Chapter Sixty-Three

Healing

Keep close attention to your body and what you truly feel is helping, continuing with those activities as much as possible. There might be supplements, treatments, or activities which can be a bit too strong at times. Pay attention to that and ease up on anything if you feel the need. Also keep in mind that things can seem like they are getting worse before they get better. When I first began many intense therapeutic activities I was feeling tired. As I paid attention to my body it was telling me it needed rest and relaxation in order for all of the healing to take place and really sink in. In addition, some of the times my gut was repairing it did feel different, a "soreness" of sorts, but I knew true healing was occurring. The GI system, as it detoxifies, can also feel like it is getting worse when it is actually doing what it needs to restore heath. Joints and other parts of the body can also feel "different" sensations as they heal. Stagnant emotions will most likely need to be released during your journey, therefore if you are feeling depressed it is okay. Just release the feelings to clear them from your mind and body, using suggestions found in this book (or from your personal therapist of course).

You may notice emotions "bubbling up" and that is all okay as well. Just allow, release, and clear them as needed.

Please always remember that true and complete health restoration usually takes time. Although we have all heard miraculous factual stories of rapid cures, it does not usually happen overnight. However, it is highly probable that you will begin feeling better quickly while the reading this book and after participating in your therapeutic activities. You will be on the path back to health! If you continue to have some symptoms, just simply begin your healing activities again (such as affirmations/meditation statements and other suggestions contained in this book). Continue until the symptom subsides. Please do not get discouraged with the process of your healing, and remember that self-care will be ongoing! Know that with alternative treatments it can take months or even years for your physical health to fully restore. Often it is correcting the underlying causes of illness, so be patient with yourself as this takes time. Always remember that we have the ability to heal, but it is sometimes a slow process, and we may not always realize when it is happening. Whenever you can, replace fearful thoughts about the future with feelings of peace, love, and joy! Let the Universe know that you are open to all healing possibilities, and then the opportunities will come to you to pursue, absorb, or allow. By reading this book you are already well on your way!

"I am constantly discovering new ways to improve my health."

~ Louise Hay

Chapter Sixty-Four

Pass it on!

P ass on the healing to others! Interestingly, having a sense of purpose has been known to lower the stress hormone cortisol in the body. This in turn increases the body's natural ability to repair itself as well as maintain optimal health. Having a sense of purpose can also lengthen your lifespan. If you have had an illness, perhaps you will find that one of your purposes in life is to help others overcome the same or similar physical, emotional, or spiritual issues that you have experienced.

"In the middle of every difficulty lies opportunity".

~ Albert Einstein

If you are, or become, a healer, and you choose to disclose what you have been though, you may receive more clients because they know you will

understand exactly what they are going through, which can facilitate the therapy.
It will also make you more approachable. This can be a gift.

"People who survive illness and hardship with an open mind and without
bitterness are frequently the best healers".

~ Kenneth Cohen

Chapter Sixty-Five

Final Thoughts

In conclusion, to any of you who perhaps have been told by Western medicine that "nothing" can be done to prevent or stop a chronic condition, or provide any real healing past just symptom-managing pharmaceuticals (which can also sometimes be toxic or have serious side effects), amazingly this book is full of that "nothing".

"Do not stay with any medical doctors who make you feel hopeless about your condition. Lupus, like all autoimmune diseases, has a high potential to go into remission. The suggestions of practitioners, for good or ill, can be powerful influences on your state of health."

~ Andrew Weil, MD

Keep talking to people who have the potential to help you or your situation. Keep reading and learning. Keep communicating to the Universe that you are open to all types of healing and allow it all to come to you.

"Never stop trying. Never stop believing. Never give up. Your day will come."

~ Mandy Hale

Like I said previously, if some folks tell me that because of this book they did not give up, then all of this writing was well worth it to me! Do not give up. The hardest part is usually the beginning. Give it ample time for all of your "puzzle pieces" to come together and your positive thoughts and visualizations to manifest. Pay attention to what your body needs and what it may be communicating. Notice all of the healing opportunities that present themselves to you. Love yourself, relax, and be sure to allow in love and goodness from all positive sources.

I truly hope you found the information in this book to be "The Blueprint for Vibrant Health" like it was for me!

Whatever you may think of this publication (and I hope you found it helpful), and regardless of the state of your physical body, the fact is that you are alive now! So, experience everything you can. None of us know how long we have here. Hug your loved ones and fully live your life in every possible positive way. Notice the beauty around you at all times. I hope you often take time out to watch the sunset, or anything that is "awe inspiring" to you, meanwhile being grateful to be alive experiencing it.

"The enlightened give thanks for what most people take for granted."

~ Michael Bernard Beckwith

About the Author

G ina L. Spielman, LCSW, C.H. is a Licensed Clinical Social Worker and a Certified Hypnotist. She has a Master's Degree and more than twenty five years of experience working in the healthcare field.

Continually attending clinical professional trainings also provides significant valuable information on effective holistic interventions, and she is a Certified Mental Health Integrative Medicine Provider as well as Certified in Natural Holistic Remedies. A personal journey with autoimmune conditions has given her first-hand knowledge of her own healing ability. The experience with her own healthcare, and all of the service providers and healers she has learned from over the years, has helped solidify her knowledge. All of that background, along with extensive research, has merged to create the life-changing book "The Blueprint for Vibrant Health".

Gina Spielman's psychotherapy practice is located near Chicago (online consultation is included). She is also the author of a book entitled "The Blueprint for a Successful Practice" and is a freelance writer. Gina lives in Illinois, with her husband and son. During her leisure time, she enjoys the outdoors whenever possible (walking, hiking, camping, geocaching), collecting crystals and stones, jewelry making, gardening, decorating, and travel with her family.

If you found this book helpful, feel free to follow "Gina L. Spielman, LCSW & Associates" on Facebook. Our page contains inspirational and educational messages, as well as any updates about our work (including future books). Check in periodically for anything new and feel free to sign up to be included on our email list. In addition, we are currently active on LinkedIn, and have begun a YouTube Channel as well as a blog. You may also email us directly with any questions or comments (or possible input for our next book) at our confidential email address: gs@ginaspielman.com. Website: www.ginaspielman.com. We encourage you to leave an honest review of this book on Amazon.com and/or on the site in which it was purchased. We also invite you to leave a review on Goodreads.com.

Acknowledgements

First and foremost, I want to sincerely thank my absolutely brilliant husband, Eric, who has helped tremendously in compiling this book, and has been wonderfully supportive throughout this entire writing process! I also want to thank all of the treatment providers and healers that have taught me so much. A few of the more current ones that come to mind are: Acupuncturist, Kurt Redmond; Acupuncturist, Laurie Stone; Massage Therapist, Rita Vargas; Reiki Master, Samantha Wood; Spiritual Clearing and Healing Facilitator, Michael Golzmane; Spiritual Counselor, Judith; and Shaman, Monica Tyler. You all are magnificent human beings and are making the world a much better place for countless people! A few that come to mind from the recent past are Dr. Erica Mennerick as well as Mary Eileen Cole, LCSW. I want to truly thank them as well.

"A great healer is one who teaches, inspires, and models how a patient can heal himself or herself."

~ Kenneth Cohen

In addition, I want to thank Racquel Valencia Hays, LCSW, CADC, Melissa Roth, Hypnotherapist, and the "Woman with Lupus" for their incredibly generous, noteworthy, and inspiring contributions to this book.

Made in United States
North Haven, CT
27 March 2023

34638651R00221